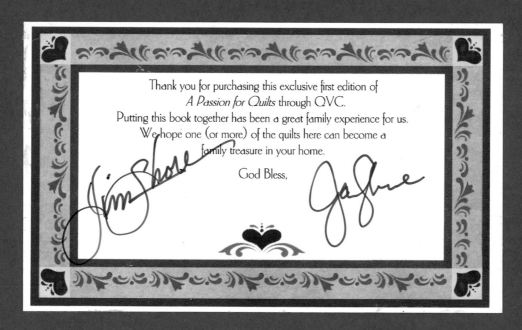

Thank you for purchasing this exclusive first edition of
A Passion for Quilts through QVC.
Putting this book together has been a great family experience for us.
We hope one (or more) of the quilts here can become a
family treasure in your home.

God Bless,

Jim & Jan Shore's

Passion for Quilts

All American **Crafts**
Publishing, Inc

Dedication

I would like to dedicate this book to the women in my life: the ones who have gone and the ones who are still here. First, to my amazing mother, who was my inspiration, my best friend, and my champion. She was a superb seamstress who instilled in me an undying love of quilts and vintage fabrics from an early age. I will love and miss her forever.

Also to my incredible sister Billie, who is a shining light and a true constant in my life. We've shared so much, done so much together through the years—all those antique and craft shows. Lots of work and masses of fun! Without her, this book would still be a dream.

And last, but by no means least, thanks to all my inspirational daughters, who constantly surprise and delight me. From them, I've learned the meaning of love and importance of family, of history, and the value of all things cherished and passed through generations. I hope to teach them the same.

Jan Shore

Jim & Jan Shore's
Passion for Quilts

Published by

All American Crafts, Inc.
7 Waterloo Road
Stanhope, NJ 07874
www.allamericancrafts.com

Publisher: **Jerry Cohen**

Chief Executive Officer: **Darren Cohen**

Product Development Director: **Brett Cohen**

Editor: **Alison Martin**

Art Director: **Kelly Alberston**

Technical Illustrator: **Rory Byra**

Style Editor: **Natalie Rhinesmith**

Photography: **Honour Hiers Photography**

                Van Zandbergen Photography

Vice President/Quilting Advertising
  & Marketing: **Carol Newman**

Printed in the USA
©2009 All American Crafts, Inc
ISBN: 978-0-9819762-0-4
Library of Congress Control Number: 2009935428

Introduction

This is not our first project together. After 20 odd years of marriage we've had our share of joint ventures, everything from raising kids to running a business to figuring out what's for dinner. We've had quite a ride together and for the most part, it's been a lot of fun. But this particular project is special because quilting has been a part of our lives for as long as we can remember. We share a love for quilts and quilters, and the influence of each in our lives has been profound.

First off, only one of us (Jan) is actually a quilter. But both our mothers were, as were their mothers before them. In fact Jim's maternal grandmother, with her crazy quilts and intricate Trapunto work, is still one of the finest quilters we've ever known. We both learned a lot living with these women—things like patience, perseverance and thrift, some of the basic attitudes essential to quilting have served us well in every part of our lives. But more than just the basics of how-to and what-it-takes, we saw in their passion for quilting an undeniable spirit of creativity and a boundless imagination, translating ordinary, mismatched bits of cloth and thread into something intricately constructed and beautiful. That passion, the desire to create something wonderful, is at the heart of quilting and is the basis of what the world calls 'folk art.'

We've always tried to keep that spirit in our own lives. When we first met, Jim was

working as a mechanical engineer. But seeing where his heart was, early on we made a commitment as a family to follow his passion, to give up engineering and do whatever it took to allow Jim the opportunity to create. It was quite a leap of faith and led to some pretty hard times. But it was also the start of a great adventure that changed our lives forever. Jim's artistry and drive fuels what we do. Our shared love of quilts and the interaction we've developed over the years provides common ground for our work and makes us both better at what we do. We've learned something in the last 20 years that quilters when they get together have understood for generations. Creativity is contagious.

Contents

 Santa's Coming to Town

My mother was a quilter, as was her mother, and *her* mother before that. I grew up around quilts and quilters and can't help but love both. And though quilts were a constant in my youth, I associate them most with Christmas. Most of the holiday decorations in our house were quilted, everything from wall hangings to throws to pillows to tablecloths to the ornaments themselves. Each piece was handmade in our home for no purpose other than to celebrate the season and add beauty to our lives. To me, that is the essence of folk art.

Jim Shore

Skill level: Intermediate
Block size sewn into quilt: 12" x 12"
Number of blocks: 12
Finished quilt size: 60" x 74"

SUPPLIES

Note: Yardage is based on 42" wide cotton fabric.
- 1/2 yd. of mottled blue
- 2/3 yd. of yellow tonal
- 3/4 yd. of purple tonal
- 3/4 yd. of green tonal
- 1 yd. of floral
- 1-1/4 yds. of white tonal
- 1-1/3 yds. of red tonal
- 68" x 82" piece of backing fabric
- 68" x 82" piece of batting
- Thread in colors to match fabrics
- Rotary cutter, ruler, and mat
- Basic sewing supplies

Every Christmas I put up seven to eight Christmas trees. One of the trees is always covered in Jim's figurines. Not just ornaments but full-size figures are wired in also. Now that I have this quilt, it will hang on the wall beside the "Jim Shore" tree. I just can't wait to see them together.

Jan Shore

CUTTING INSTRUCTIONS

From the mottled blue, cut:
Five 2-1/2" x 42" strips (for inner border)

From the yellow tonal, cut:
Two 5-1/4" x 42" strips; recut into twelve 5-1/4"
   squares, then cut diagonally in half *twice*
Two 4-1/2" x 42" strips; recut into twelve
   4-1/2" squares

From the purple tonal, cut:
Seven 2-1/2" x 42" strips (for outer border)
Three 1-1/2" x 42" strips (for sashing squares)

From the green tonal, cut:
Seven 2-1/2" x 42" strips (for binding)
Three 1-1/2" x 42" strips (for sashing squares)

From the floral, cut:
Six 4-1/2" x 42" strips (for middle border)
Eight 2-1/2" squares

From the white tonal, cut:
Two 5-1/4" x 42" strips; recut into twelve 5-1/4"
   squares, then cut diagonally in half *twice*
Six 4-1/2" x 42" strips; recut into forty-eight 4-1/2"
   squares

From the red tonal, cut:
Two 12-1/2" x 42" strips; recut into thirty-one
   2-1/2" x 12-1/2" strips (for sashing)
Three 5-1/4" x 42" strips; recut into twenty-four
   5-1/4" squares, then cut diagonally in half *twice*

INSTRUCTIONS

Note: Use a 1/4" seam allowance throughout. Press
seams toward the darker fabric after adding each
piece or as indicated.

Ohio Star Block Assembly

1. Following **Diagram 1**, sew a 5-1/4" red tonal
triangle to a 5-1/4" white tonal triangle. Make a total
of 48 units. In the same manner, make a total of 48
units using red tonal triangles and yellow tonal triangles. Stitch a red/white unit to a red/yellow unit to
make one star point unit. Make a total of 48 units.

Make 48

Make 48

Make 48
Diagram 1

2. Referring to the **Block Diagrams**, sew four star
point units together with one 4-1/2" yellow tonal
square and four 4-1/2" white tonal squares to make
one 12-1/2" x 12-1/2" block. Make a total of 12
blocks.

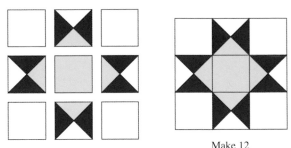
Make 12
Block Diagrams

Quilt Assembly and Finishing

1. *Sashing squares*. Following **Diagram 2** and
using 1-1/2" x 42" strips, sew a purple tonal strip
lengthwise to a green tonal strip. Repeat to make
three strip sets. Crosscut seventy-two 1-1/2" wide
segments. Stitch two segments together as shown in
Diagram 3. Make a total of 36 units. Set aside 16
units for use in the borders.

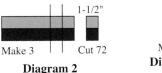
Make 3   Cut 72   Make 36
Diagram 2   **Diagram 3**
1-1/2"

2. *Sashing rows*. Referring to the **Quilt Layout
Diagram**, sew four sashing squares alternately
together with three 2-1/2" x 12-1/2" red tonal strips.
Make a total of five sashing rows.

3. *Block rows*. Stitch three blocks alternately
together with four 2-1/2" x 12-1/2" red tonal strips.
Make a total of four block rows.

4. Sew the sashing rows alternately together with
the block rows to complete the 44-1/2" x 58-1/2"
quilt center.

5. *Inner border*. Stitch the five 2-1/2" x 42" mottled blue strips short ends together to make one long
strip. Cut two 44-1/2" lengths and two 58-1/2"
lengths. Sew the shorter strips to the short sides of
the quilt center. Stitch a unit set aside in step 1 to
each end of the longer strips, then sew to the other
sides.

6. *Middle border*. Using the **Quilt Layout Diagram** for reference, stitch two units set aside in step
1 together with two 2-1/2" floral squares. Make a
total of four cornerstones. Sew the six 4-1/2" x 42"
floral strips short ends together to make one long
strip. Cut two 48-1/2" lengths and two 62-1/2"

lengths. Stitch the shorter strips to the short sides of the quilt top. Sew a cornerstone to each end of the longer strips, then stitch to the other sides.

7. *Outer border.* Sew the seven 2-1/2" x 42" purple tonal strips short ends together to make one long strip. Cut two 56-1/2" lengths and two 70-1/2" lengths. Stitch the shorter strips to the short sides of the quilt top. Sew a unit set aside in step 1 to each end of the longer strips, then stitch to the other sides.

8. Layer the quilt top right side up on top of the batting and the wrong side of the backing. Quilt as desired. Trim backing and batting even with the quilt top.

9. Bind as desired using the seven 2-1/2" x 42" green tonal strips.

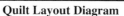

Quilt Layout Diagram

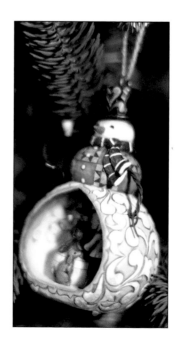

Jim Shore's hand drawing of quilt. ©JSHORE

Designed by Kathy Atwell and Jan Shore • **Pieced by Alison Newman** • **Finished quilt size:** 60" x 74"

An Eerie Eve Awaits

I had a recurring nightmare as a kid where I was stalked by a pumpkin-headed goblin out to snatch my life and steal my soul. Who knows why. Maybe I was too young when I saw some Disney movie or read "Sleepy Hollow." But the truth is, I was more or less terrified of jack-o-lanterns for a long time. I only really got my fear under control when I began to draw that pumpkin guy, incorporating him into my art. Now that I consciously create him I've grown to love him. He's got a lovable mischief that sparks the imagination and speaks to the fun-loving side of Halloween.

Jim Shore

Our Halloween would not be complete without Pumpkin Head, who is Jim's childhood nemesis. As a little boy, Pumpkin Head was always outside waiting for him. Now Pumpkin Head has become a favorite friend to Jim, and is always lurking somewhere around our house. Halloween is my second favorite season. We've started having a Halloween party every year. But with our family any excuse to get together will do. This piece would also be great as a bench cover.

Jan Shore

17

Skill level: Intermediate
Finished runner size: Approx. 18" x 66"
Finished placemat size: 12" x 18"

SUPPLIES

Note: Yardage is based on 42" wide cotton fabric. Enough yardage is included to make the runner and four placemats.
- 1/8 yd. of yellow tonal
- 1/4 yd. of green print
- 5/8 yd. of purple print
- 2/3 yd. of mottled lavender
- 1 yd. of mottled deep purple
- 1 yd. of orange print
- 24" x 72" piece of backing fabric (for runner)
- Four 18" x 24" pieces of backing fabric (for placemats)
- 24" x 72" piece of batting (for runner)
- Four 18" x 24" pieces of batting (for placemats)
- 1/4 yd. of 18" wide fusible web
- White chalk pencil
- Thread in colors to match fabrics
- Rotary cutter, ruler, and mat
- Basic sewing and pressing supplies

CUTTING INSTRUCTIONS

From the green print, cut:
Two 2" x 42" strips; recut into ten 2" x 6" pieces and four 2" x 5-1/2" pieces

From the purple print, cut:
Four 3-7/8" x 42" strips; recut into thirty-two 3-7/8" squares

From the mottled lavender, cut:
Five 3-7/8" x 42" strips; recut into forty-six 3-7/8" squares

From the mottled deep purple, cut:
Eight 3-7/8" x 42" strips; recut into seventy-eight 3-7/8" squares

From the orange print, cut:
One 9" x 42" strip; recut into two 9" squares
One 8" x 42" strip; recut into four 8" squares
Seven 2" x 42" strips; recut into eight 2" x 15-1/2" strips and eight 2" x 12-1/2" strips (for placemats)

INSTRUCTIONS

Note: Use a 1/4" seam allowance throughout. Press seams toward the darker fabric after adding each piece or as indicated.

Runner Assembly and Finishing

1. Draw a diagonal line on the wrong side of each 3-7/8" mottled deep purple square using the white chalk pencil. Following **Diagram 1**, place a marked square right sides together with a 3-7/8" mottled lavender square. Sew 1/4" away from each side of the drawn line, cut apart on the line, and press open. Make a total of 92 lavender units. Set aside 32 units for the placemats.

Make 92

Diagram 1

2. Stitch six units together as shown in **Diagram 2** to make one row. Make a total of ten rows. Sew five rows together as shown to make a lavender section. Repeat to make a second section.

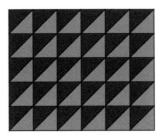

Make 2

Diagram 2

3. Place a marked square right sides together with a 3-7/8" purple print square. Stitch 1/4" away from each side of the drawn line, cut apart on the line, and press open. Make a total of 64 purple units. Set aside 28 units for the placemats.

4. Sew six units together to make one row (see **Diagram 3**). Make a total of six rows. Stitch the rows together to make the purple section.

Diagram 3

5. Referring to the **Runner Layout Diagram**, sew a lavender section to top and bottom of the purple section to complete the 18-1/2" x 48-1/2" runner center.

6. Following **Diagram 4**, mark 2" on each side of three corners of each 8" orange print square. Trim from mark to mark on each corner to angle. Mark 2-1/2" on each side of each corner on the two 9" orange print squares. Trim from mark to mark on each corner to angle.

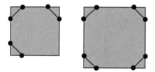

Diagram 4

7. Stitch a 2" x 6" green print strip to the straight bottom edge of each trimmed 8" orange print square as shown in **Diagram 5**. Trim the strips even with the angled corner. Center and sew a 2" x 5-1/2" green print strip to the angled bottom corner of the squares. Trim the strips even with the bottom of the green strips and the edge of the orange squares to complete two small pumpkins and two reverse small pumpkins.

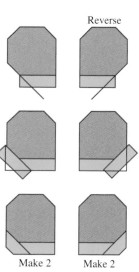

Reverse

Make 2   Make 2

Diagram 5

8. Turn the top angled corners and top straight edge of each pumpkin under 1/4". Press. Place a small pumpkin on the left edge of one end of the runner center, with the top of the pumpkin 1" from the top of the bottom row of lavender units and the left edge aligned with the edge of the runner center (see **Diagram 6**). Pin in place. Attach a reverse small pumpkin to the right edge of the runner center in the same manner. Repeat for the other end of the runner center. Stitch the top edge of the pumpkins in place using matching thread.

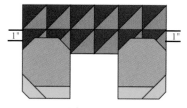

1"   1"

Diagram 6

9. Using the patterns provided, trace the indicated number of shapes onto the paper side of the fusible web, leaving at least 1/2" between shapes. Cut out roughly. Following manufacturer's directions, fuse the shapes onto the wrong side of the fabrics designated on the patterns. Cut out neatly. Referring to the photo for placement, remove the paper backing and arrange the shapes on the small pumpkins. Fuse in place. Set aside the remaining shapes for the large pumpkins. Stitch all shapes in place using matching thread.

Runner Layout Diagram

10. Following **Diagram 7**, center and sew a 2" x 6" green print strip to the bottom of each trimmed 9" orange print square. Trim the strips even with the angled corners. Center and stitch a 2" x 6" green print strip to the angled bottom corners of the squares. Trim the strips even to complete the large pumpkins.

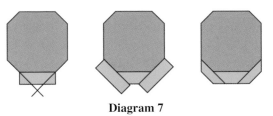

Diagram 7

11. Turn the top and side edges under 1/4". Press. Center a large pumpkin on each end of the runner center as shown in **Diagram 8** with the top edge approximately 2" from the top of the bottom row of lavender units and the top of the green side strips on the large pumpkin aligned with the green strips of the small pumpkins. Pin in place. Sew the turned-under edges in place using matching thread. Unfold the green strip edges that are not stitched down and press flat.

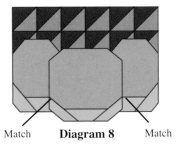

Match   **Diagram 8**   Match

12. Arrange the remaining appliqué shapes on the large pumpkins and fuse in place. Sew the shapes in place using matching thread.

13. Layer the runner top wrong side up on top of the right side of the runner backing and the runner batting. Pin the layers together. Stitch around the outside edge through all layers, leaving an 8" opening on one long side. Trim the outside corners and clip the inside corners. Turn right side out. Press edges flat. Turn the opening edges 1/4" to the inside. Hand stitch the opening closed. Quilt as desired.

Placemat Assembly and Finishing

1. Following **Diagram 9**, sew seven leftover purple units and eight leftover lavender units together into three horizontal rows of five units each. Stitch the rows together to complete one 9-1/2" x 15-1/2" placemat center.

Diagram 9

2. Referring to the **Placemat Layout Diagram**, sew a 2" x 15-1/2" orange print strip to each long side of the placemat center. Stitch the 2" x 12-1/2" orange print strips to the short sides.

3. Layer the placemat top wrong side up on top of the right side of a placemat backing and batting. Pin the layers together. Sew around the outside edge through all layers, leaving an 8" opening on one long side. Trim backing and batting even with runner top. Trim the outside corners and clip the inside corners. Turn right side out. Press edges flat. Turn the opening edges 1/4" to the inside. Hand stitch the opening closed. Quilt as desired.

4. Repeat steps 1 through 3 to make a total of four placemats.

Make 4

Placemat Layout Diagram

Jim Shore's hand drawing of table runner. ©JSHORE

Jim Shore's hand drawing of placemat. ©JSHORE

21

Designed by Jan Shore • Pieced by Lynn Baker • Finished runner size: Approx. 18" x 66"

Finished placemat size: 12" x 18"

Three Little Pigs

I've always been fascinated by the idea of composition in quilting, the combination of color and pattern to create a mood, an emotion, or a sense of place. Certain combinations evoke an occasion like a wedding, others a place like home. Some are feminine and others just for kids. But the best compositions are dynamic: they keep the eye moving from place to place around the entire piece. That's what I strive for in my work. I look at one of my pieces and if my eye stops on a particular pattern or color, I know I've got changes to make.

Jim Shore

Jim's nursery rhyme collection is so cute. It was very difficult to choose just one of them to use. But I wanted something that would be for little boys, so I chose the Three Little Pigs. All three of the pigs donated to this design, and for this I thank them. The guys fit in great with some of my other collections. I love old children's toys, from tin to plastic Cracker Jack toys.

Jan Shore

Skill level: Beginner
Block size sewn into quilt: 4" x 4"
Number of blocks: 26
Finished quilt size: 40" x 44"

SUPPLIES

Note: Yardage is based on 42" wide cotton fabric.
- 1/4 yd. of green tonal
- 3/8 yd. of light blue print
- 3/8 yd. of dark blue print
- 1/2 yd. of pink tonal
- 1/2 yd. of cream tonal
- 2/3 yd. of green print
- 3/4 yd. of red tonal
- 46" x 50" piece of backing fabric
- 46" x 50" piece of batting
- Thread in colors to match fabrics
- Rotary cutter, ruler, and mat
- Basic sewing supplies

CUTTING INSTRUCTIONS

From the green tonal, cut:
Two 2-1/2" x 42" strips

From the light blue print, cut:
Four 2-1/2" x 42" strips

From the dark blue print, cut:
Four 2-1/2" x 42" strips

From the pink tonal, cut:
Four 2-7/8" x 42" strips; recut into fifty-two
 2-7/8" squares

From the cream tonal, cut:
Four 2-7/8" x 42" strips; recut into fifty-two
 2-7/8" squares

From the green print, cut:
Two 2-1/2" x 42" strips
Five 2-1/4" x 42" strips (for binding)

From the red tonal, cut:
Nine 2-1/2" x 42" strips; recut each of two strips into
 one 24-1/2" length and one 12-1/2" length; recut
 one strip into two 20-1/2" lengths; recut each of
 two strips into one 32-1/2" length (set aside
 remainder); recut each of two strips into one
 36-1/2" length
Sew a remainder to each of two remaining strips,
 then trim to measure 44-1/2"

INSTRUCTIONS

Note: Use a 1/4" seam allowance throughout. Press
seams toward the darker fabric after adding each
piece or as indicated.

Quilt Center Assembly

1. Following **Diagram 1** sew two 2-1/2" x 42"
green print strips lengthwise together with two
2-1/2" x 42" green tonal strips.

Diagram 1

2. Cut the strip set in half widthwise to yield two
21" long units. Stitch the units lengthwise together as
shown in **Diagram 2** to make one 16-1/2" wide strip
set. Cut six 2-1/2" wide segments.

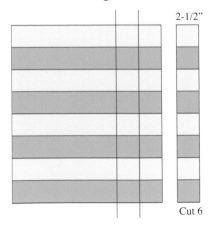

Cut 6

Diagram 2

3. Referring to the **Quilt Layout Diagram** and noting orientation, sew the segments together vertically to complete the 12-1/2" x 16-1/2" quilt center.

Pinwheel Block Assembly

1. Draw a diagonal line on the wrong side of each 2-7/8" pink tonal square. Following **Diagram 3**, place a marked square right sides together with a 2-7/8" cream tonal square. Sew 1/4" away from each side of the drawn line, then cut apart along the line. Trim to measure 2-1/2" x 2-1/2". Make a total of 104 half-square triangle units.

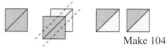

Make 104

Diagram 3

2. Referring to the **Block Diagram** and noting orientation, stitch four half-square triangle units together to make one 4-1/2" x 4-1/2" pinwheel block. Make a total of 26 blocks.

Make 26

Block Diagram

Quilt Assembly and Finishing

1. *First border.* Referring to the **Quilt Layout Diagram**, sew the 2-1/2" x 12-1/2" red tonal strips to the short sides of the quilt center and the 2-1/2" x 20-1/2" red tonal strips to the long sides.

Quilt Layout Diagram

2. *Second (pieced) border.* Stitch five pinwheel blocks together to make one pieced strip. Repeat to make a second strip, then sew to the long sides of the quilt top. Stitch six pinwheel blocks together, then repeat to make a second strip. Sew to the other sides of the quilt top.

3. *Third border.* Stitch the 2-1/2" x 24-1/2" red tonal strips to the short sides of the quilt top and the 2-1/2" x 32-1/2" red tonal strips to the other sides.

4. *Fourth (pieced) border.* Following **Diagram 4** and using 2-1/2" x 42" strips, sew a dark blue print strip lengthwise to a light blue print strip. Make a

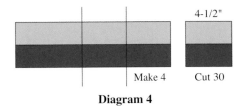

4-1/2"

Make 4   Cut 30

Diagram 4

total of four strip sets. Crosscut thirty 4-1/2" wide segments. Stitch eight segments together as shown in the **Quilt Layout Diagram** to make one pieced strip. Repeat to make a second strip, then sew to the long sides of the quilt top. Stitch seven segments together to make one pieced strip. Repeat to make a second strip. Sew a pinwheel block to each end of these strips, then stitch to the other sides of the quilt top.

5. *Fifth border.* Sew the 2-1/2" x 36-1/2" red tonal strips to the short sides of the quilt top and the 2-1/2" x 44-1/2" red tonal strips to the other sides.

6. Layer the quilt top right side up on top of the batting and the wrong side of the backing. Quilt as desired. Trim backing and batting even with the quilt top.

7. Bind as desired using the five 2-1/2" x 42" green print strips.

Jim Shore's hand drawing of quilt. ©JSHORE

Designed by Jan Shore • **Pieced by Jenny Vandersnick** • **Finished quilt size:** 40" x 44"

May the Road Rise Up to Meet You

My Dad used to say, "I'm not Irish and I don't associate with those that are." Of course he married my mother, a proud Irish woman, so his bark was obviously worse than his bite. My angels always carry a hint, a smile, expression, or feature of the important women in my life, mostly my wife Jan or one of my daughters. This Irish angel is especially dear to me and patterned after my mother. She was a wonderful quilter, and in my mind, a great artist in her own right. She often used the Irish chain, a reminder, I suppose, of the home of our ancestors.

Jim Shore

Skill level: Intermediate
Block size sewn into quilt: 6" x 6", 4" x 6"
Number of blocks: 12, 12, 13
Finished quilt size: Approx. 62" x 62"

SUPPLIES

Note: Yardage is based on 42" wide cotton fabric.
- 1/2 yd. of light green tonal
- 7/8 yd. of purple tonal
- 1 yd. of mottled dark green
- 1-5/8 yd. of red tonal
- 3-1/2 yds. of solid cream
- 68" x 68" piece of backing fabric
- 68" x 68" piece of batting
- 1 yd. of 18" wide fusible web
- Thread in colors to match fabrics
- Rotary cutter, ruler, and mat
- Template plastic
- Basic sewing and pressing supplies
- Bias bar

Jim and I love Ireland. If I were ever forced (and I would have to be forced) to live in another country it would be Ireland, hands down. From the castles to the farm cottages, its beauty knows no bounds. The people are amazing. The only thing is that they drive on the wrong side of the road. And the sheep do not obey the sheep crossing signs.

Jan Shore

31

CUTTING INSTRUCTIONS

From the purple tonal, cut:
One 26" x 42" piece (for bias binding)

From the mottled dark green, cut:
Eight 2-1/2" x 42" strips (for strip sets)
Three 2-1/2" x 42" strips; recut into thirty-six
   2-1/2" squares

From the red tonal, cut:
Two 26" x 42" strips

From the solid cream, cut:
Seven 2-1/2" x 42" strips (for strip sets)
Three 2-1/2" x 42" strips; recut into twenty-four
   2-1/2" x 4-1/2" pieces
Ten 2-1/2" x 42" strips; recut into sixty 2-1/2" x
   6-1/2" pieces
One 4-1/2" x 42" strip; recut into four 4-1/2" squares
Four 6-1/2" x 42" strips; recut into eight 4-1/2" x
   6-1/2" pieces and thirteen 6-1/2" squares
Six 6-1/2" x 42" strips (for border)

INSTRUCTIONS

Note: Use a 1/4" seam allowance throughout. Press seams toward the darker fabric after adding each piece or as indicated.

Nine-Patch Block Assembly

1. Following **Diagram 1** and using 2-1/2" x 42" strips, sew a solid cream strip lengthwise between two mottled dark green strips. Repeat to make a total of three strip sets. Crosscut thirty-six 2-1/2" wide segments. In the same manner, stitch a mottled dark green strip between two solid cream strips. Make a second strip set. Crosscut twenty-four 2-1/2" wide segments.

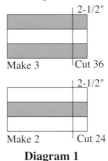

Make 3   Cut 36

Make 2   Cut 24

Diagram 1

2. Referring to the **Nine-Patch Block Diagrams**, sew a cream/green/cream segment between two green/cream/green segments to make one 6-1/2" x 6-1/2" block. Make a total of 12 blocks.

To make the partial blocks, stitch a cream/green/cream segment lengthwise to a green/cream/green segment. Make a total of 12 partial blocks.

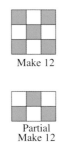

Make 12

Partial
Make 12

**Nine-Patch Block
Diagrams**

Appliqué Block Assembly

1. Trace 13 clover shapes onto the paper side of the fusible web, leaving at least 1/2" between shapes. Following manufacturer's directions, fuse the shapes onto the wrong side of the fabrics designated on the patterns. Cut out neatly.

2. Referring to the **Quilt Layout Diagram** for placement, remove the paper backing and center a clover shape on each 6-1/2" solid cream square. Fuse in place. Stitch all shapes in place using matching thread.

Row Assembly

1. *Row A.* Following **Diagram 2**, sew three partial Nine-Patch blocks together with two 4-1/2" solid cream squares, six 2-1/2" x 4-1/2" solid cream pieces, and two 4-1/2" x 6-1/2" solid cream pieces. Make a total of two A rows.

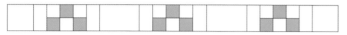

Diagram 2 Row A Make 2

2. *Row B.* Stitch six 2-1/2" mottled dark green squares together with two 2-1/2" x 4-1/2" solid cream pieces and five 2-1/2" x 6-1/2" solid cream pieces as shown in **Diagram 3**. Make a total of six B rows.

Diagram 3 Row B Make 6

3. *Row C.* Sew two Nine-Patch blocks together with two partial Nine-Patch blocks, three appliqué blocks, and six 2-1/2" x 61/2" solid cream pieces (see **Diagram 4**). Make a total of three C rows.

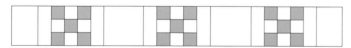

Diagram 4 Row C Make 3

4. *Row D.* Referring to **Diagram 5**, stitch three Nine-Patch blocks together with two appliqué blocks, two 4-1/2" x 6-1/2" solid cream pieces, and six 2-1/2" x 6-1/2" solid cream pieces. Make a total of two D rows.

Diagram 5 Row D Make 2

Quilt Assembly and Finishing

1. Referring to the **Quilt Layout Diagram**, sew the rows together to complete the 50-1/2" x 50-1/2" quilt center.

2. *Border.* Stitch the six 6-1/2" x 42" solid cream strips short ends together to make one long strip. Cut two 50-1/2" lengths and two 62-1/2" lengths. Sew the shorter strips to the top and bottom of the quilt center and the longer strips to the sides. Press seams toward the border.

3. Using the patterns provided, create a side scallop and corner scallop template. Mark the scallops (five full scallops per side, and four corner scallops) on the cream border strips, aligning the outer curves of the scallops with the outer edge of the border strips. Referring to **Diagram 6**, trim one end of the 26" x 42" red strips at a 45° angle. Cut 1-1/2" wide bias strips to total 540". Join the strips on the short ends. Fold the strip in half along the length with right side out. Stitch along the raw edges using a *scant* 1/4" seam allowance. Trim the seam allowance to 1/8". Flatten the strip with the seam centered on one side. Insert the bias bar into the strip and press the strip flat to make the border vine piece. Referring to the photo for placement and echoing the marked scallops on the borders, arrange and pin the red vine along the cream border. Trim excess at the end leaving 1/4" to turn in on one end. Turn 1/4" in on one end, and cover the raw edge of the remaining end. Stitch in place as desired using thread to match fabric.

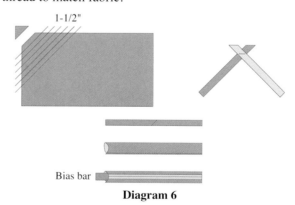

Diagram 6

1-1/2"

Bias bar

4. Layer the quilt top right side up on top of the batting and the wrong side of the backing. Quilt as desired. Sew the scallops on the marked lines to keep the layers from shifting, but do not quilt beyond the marked edge. Trim backing and batting even with the quilt top.

5. Following **Diagram 6**, trim one end of the 26" x 42" purple tonal piece at a 45° angle. Cut enough 2-1/4" wide bias strips to total 288" when sewn together. Stitch the strips short ends together to make one long strip. Press seams open. Press the binding strip in half lengthwise with wrong sides together. Align the edge of the binding with the scallop border and begin sewing 1/4" seam at the top of one scallop. Stitch to the base of the V, stopping with the needle down. Lift the presser foot, pivot the quilt and binding, then sew out of the V, being careful not to sew any pleats. Continue working around the quilt, easing the binding around the curves. Trim seam allowance even with the edge of the binding. Turn the binding to the back and stitch by hand, allowing the inside corners to fold over on themselves.

Jim Shore's hand drawing of quilt. ©JSHORE

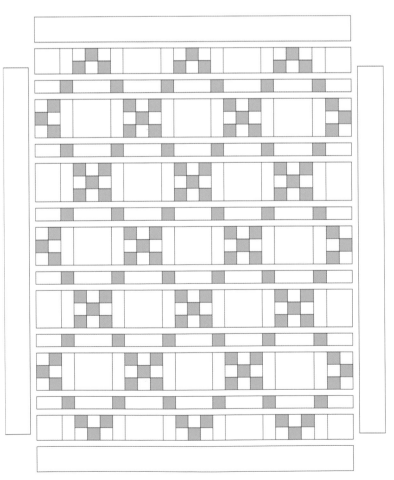

Quilt Layout Diagram

Designed by Jan Shore • **Pieced by Judy Neal** • **Finished quilt size:** Approx. 62" x 62"

Over the River

I have a friend who makes fabulous miniature sleighs. They are true works of art, hand crafted out of metal and wood to be exact replicas down to the last detail. The runners are perfectly shaped for cutting through snow, the buckles and hardware are weighty and functional, and the wood chassis are proportioned for comfort and speed. I could spend hours admiring the beauty and intricacy of his work. There's a passion to it, a real commitment that captures the romance of his subject matter. It's the same passion and romance I try to bring to my own art.

Jim Shore

Skill level: Beginner
Finished runner size: 16" x 64"
Finished placemat size: 12" x 20"

SUPPLIES

Note: Yardage is based on 42" wide cotton fabric. Enough yardage is included to make the runner and four placemats.

- Scraps of light red tonal
- Scraps of mottled dark red
- 1/4 yd. of cream print
- 3/8 yd. of solid teal
- 1/2 yd. of mottled purple
- 7/8 yd. of green print
- 1 yd. of green tonal
- 22" x 74" piece of backing fabric (for runner)
- Four 18" x 26" pieces of backing fabric (for placemats)
- 2" x 74" piece of batting (for runner)
- Four 18" x 26" pieces of batting (for placemats)
- 1/4 yd. of 18" wide fusible web
- Thread in colors to match fabrics
- Rotary cutter, ruler, and mat
- White chalk pencil
- Basic sewing and pressing supplies

As a little girl I loved the song "Over the River and Through the Woods." The song always made me think of hopping in a sleigh and traveling off for the holidays, snuggled up in a quilt with my favorite pillow, and waking up just in time to see my grandmother standing at her door to greet us. And it's all true, except for the sleigh. I think I was really snuggled in a 1967 Chevy.

Jan Shore

37

CUTTING INSTRUCTIONS

From the cream print, cut:
One 6-1/2" x 42" strip; recut into two 6-1/2" x
16-1/2" strips

From the solid teal, cut:
Two 4-7/8" x 42" strips; recut into twelve
4-7/8" squares

From the mottled purple, cut:
Four 2-1/2" x 42" strips; recut into eight 2-1/2" x
12-1/2" strips
Two 1-1/2" x 42" strips; recut into four 1-1/2" x
16-1/2" strips

From the green print, cut:
Five 4-7/8" x 42" strips; recut into thirty-six
4-7/8" squares

From the green tonal, cut:
Six 4-7/8" x 42" strips; recut into forty-eight
4-7/8" squares

INSTRUCTIONS

Note: Use a 1/4" seam allowance throughout. Press
seams toward the darker fabric after adding each
piece or as indicated.

Runner Assembly and Finishing

1. Draw a diagonal line on the wrong side of
each of the 4-7/8" green tonal squares. Following
Diagram 1, place the marked squares right sides
together with the 4-7/8" green print squares and
4-7/8" solid teal squares. Sew 1/4" away from each
side of the drawn lines, then cut apart on the lines
and trim to yield 72 green print units and 24 teal
units. Set aside 36 green units and 12 teal units for
the placemats.

Make 72 Make 24
Diagram 1

2. Referring to the **Block
Diagram** and noting orientation,
stitch four units together to make
one 8-1/2" x 8-1/2" block. Make
a total of 12 blocks.

Make 12
Block Diagram

3. Sew the blocks together in pairs as shown in the
Runner Layout Diagram. Stitch the pairs together
to complete the 16-1/2" x 48-1/2" runner center.

4. *Border.* Sew a 6-1/2" x 16-1/2" cream print
strip lengthwise between two 1-1/2" x 16-1/2" mottled purple strips. Repeat to make a second strip set,
then stitch to the short ends of the runner center.

5. *Appliqué.* Using the patterns provided, trace the
indicated number of appliqué shapes onto the paper
side of the fusible web, leaving at least 1/2" between
shapes. (**Note:** For reverse pieces, place the templates face down and then trace.) Cut out roughly.
Following manufacturer's directions, fuse the shapes
onto the wrong side of the fabrics designated on the
patterns. Cut out neatly. Referring to the photo for
placement, arrange the shapes on the cream border
strips. Fuse in place. Stitch all shapes in place using
matching thread.

6. Layer the runner top wrong side up on top of
the right side of the runner backing and batting. Pin
the layers together. Sew around the outside edge
through all layers, leaving an 8" opening on one long
side. Trim the outside corners and clip the inside
corners. Turn right side out. Press edges flat. Turn
the opening edges 1/4" to the inside. Hand stitch the
opening closed. Quilt as desired.

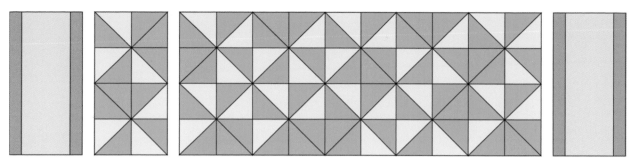

Runner Layout Diagram

Placemat Assembly and Finishing

1. Referring to the **Placemat Layout Diagram**, sew 12 of the remaining half-square triangle units together as desired into four horizontal rows of three units each. Stitch the rows together to complete the 12-1/2" x 16-1/2" placemat center. Make a total of four centers.

2. *Border*. Sew a 2-1/2" x 12-1/2" mottled purple strip to each short side of the placemat centers.

3. Layer each placemat wrong side up on top of the right side of the placemat backing and batting. Pin the layers together. Stitch around the outside edge through all layers, leaving an 6" opening on one long side. Trim the outside corners and clip the inside corners. Turn right side out. Press edges flat. Turn the opening edges 1/4" to the inside. Hand stitch the opening closed. Quilt as desired.

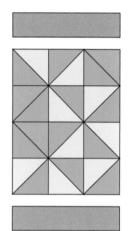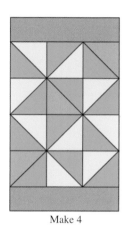

Make 4

Placemat Layout Diagram

Designed by Kathy Atwell • Pieced by Lynn Baker • Finished runner size: 16" x 64"

Jim Shore's hand drawing of runner. ©JSHORE

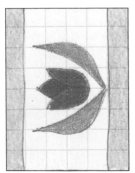

Jim Shore's hand
drawing of runner tulip
design. ©JSHORE

Jim Shore's hand drawing of placemat. ©JSHORE

Finished placemat size: 12" x 20"

Noah's Ark

The Noah's Ark that this quilt was patterned after is one of my favorite pieces that Jim has made. I really like the farm aspect of it. The quilt is just amazing. It is a very bold quilt, and would look great in any color you choose. Make it yours!

Jan Shore

I've always felt a connection to the story of Noah's Ark. It could be because I love boats. Or animals. Or the promise of a rainbow. But certainly it's because Noah's story is a story of hope—a chance to rebuild based on a new understanding of God. I've designed hundreds of Noah's Arks over the years, and each one contains some form of eight-pointed star. I've always associated stars with hope and the promise of heaven. And they're a heckuva lot easier to piece together than a rainbow.

Jim Shore

43

Skill level: Intermediate
Block size sewn into quilt: 18" x 18"
Number of blocks: 12
Finished quilt size: 75" x 93"

SUPPLIES

Note: Yardage is based on 42" wide cotton fabric.

- 2/3 yd. of green tonal
- 1-1/4 yds. of blue tonal
- 2-1/4 yds. of gold print
- 2-1/4 yds. of mottled cream
- 2-1/4 yds. of red tonal
- 83" x 101" piece of backing fabric
- 83" x 101" piece of batting
- 3 yds. of 18" wide fusible web
- Thread in colors to match fabrics
- Rotary cutter, ruler, and mat
- Template plastic
- Basic sewing and pressing supplies

CUTTING INSTRUCTIONS

From the blue tonal, cut:
Nine 2-1/4" x 42" strips (for binding)
Eight 2" x 42" strips (for outer border)

From the gold print, cut:
Four 9-1/2" x 72-1/2" *lengthwise* strips (for inner border)

From each of the mottled cream and red tonal, cut:
Five 6-1/2" x 42" strips; recut into thirty 6-1/2" squares
Six 6-1/2" x 42" strips (for templates)

INSTRUCTIONS

Note: Use a 1/4" seam allowance throughout. Press seams toward the darker fabric after adding each piece or as indicated. Trace the patterns for pieces A and B onto template plastic, then cut out neatly and label.

Sun Rays Block Assembly

1. Prepare templates for pieces A and B using the patterns provided. Cut 24 A pieces from the 6-1/2" x 42" red tonal strips and 24 A pieces from the 6-1/2" x 42" mottled cream strips. Cut 24 B pieces from the red tonal strips, then reverse the template and cut 24 reverse B (Br) pieces. Repeat to cut 24 B pieces and 24 reverse B (Br) pieces from the mottled cream strips.

2. *Cream blocks.* Referring to the **Block Diagrams**, sew a red piece B to one angled side of a cream piece A, then stitch a red piece Br to the other angled side. Press. Make a total of 24 units. Noting orientation, sew a unit to each of two opposite sides of a 6-1/2"

mottled cream square to complete the center section. Press seams toward the units. Stitch a unit between two 6-1/2" mottled cream squares. Repeat to make a second section, then sew to the top and bottom of the center section to complete one block. Press seams toward the center section. Make a total of six cream blocks.

3. *Red blocks*. Repeat steps 1 and 2 to make a total of six red blocks, this time using the red A pieces, 6-1/2" red tonal squares, cream B pieces, and cream

Br pieces. Press seams toward the red squares and away from the center section.

Quilt Assembly and Finishing

1. Referring to the **Quilt Layout Diagram**, sew the red blocks and cream blocks alternately together into four horizontal rows of three blocks each. Stitch the rows together to complete the 54-1/2" x 72-1/2" quilt center.

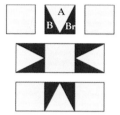

Make 6

Make 6

Block Diagrams

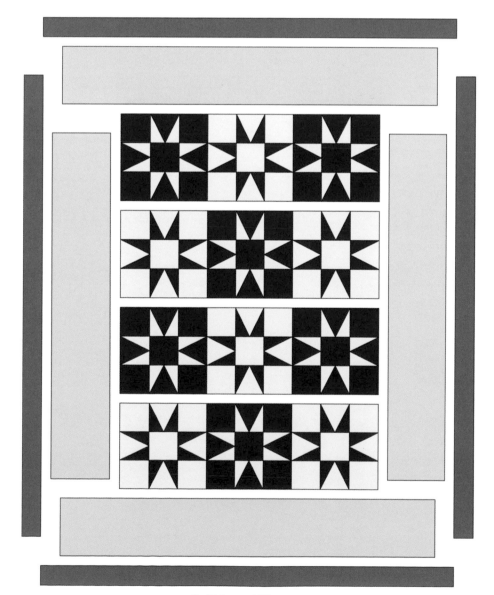

Quilt Layout Diagram

2. *Inner border.* Sew a 9-1/2" x 72-1/2" gold print strip to each long side of the quilt center. Press seams away from the quilt center. Stitch the remaining 9-1/2" x 72-1/2" strips to the top and bottom. Press seams away from the quilt center.

3. *Outer border.* Sew the eight 2" x 42" blue tonal strips short ends together to make one long strip. Press seams to one side. Cut two 90-1/2" lengths and two 75-1/2" lengths. Stitch the longer strips to the long sides of the quilt top and the shorter strips to the top and bottom. Press seams away from the quilt center.

4. *Appliqués.* Cut an 8" x 18" piece from the fusible web. Following manufacturer's directions, fuse onto the wrong side of the green tonal fabric. Cut eighteen 5/8" x 9" strips from the fused fabric for the stems. Using the patterns provided, trace the indicated number of appliqué shapes onto the paper side of the fusible web, leaving at least 1/2" between shapes. Cut out roughly. Fuse the flowers onto the wrong side of the remaining red tonal fabric and the leaves onto the wrong side of the remaining green tonal fabric. Cut out neatly. Referring to the photo for placement, remove the paper backing and arrange the shapes on the inner border. Fuse in place. Stitch all shapes in place using matching thread.

5. Layer the quilt top right side up on top of the batting and the wrong side of the backing. Quilt as desired. Trim backing and batting even with the quilt top.

6. Bind as desired using the nine 2-1/4" x 42" blue tonal strips.

Jim Shore's hand drawing of quilt. ©JSHORE

Designed by Jim and Jan Shore • Pieced by Pine Tree Country Quilts • Finished quilt size: 75" x 93"

 Home

I combine a lot of different folk art forms in my work. There are those who'll tell you that's because I can't ever stick to one thing. I like to think it's because I appreciate variety in life. And I love the comparison and contrast these different forms bring to my art. There's a real energy in the juxtaposition of the geometric precision of quilting, the delicate shapes of brush strokes in rosemaling and the primitive lines of zero perspective landscape art. It keeps the eye moving and the mind wandering over the entire composition.

Jim Shore

This quilt is really special to me. I have always loved Jim's folk art villages. Just the simplicity of the scene to me is as pretty as you will see any-where. It takes me back to another era. Wouldn't it be great to wake up here? No phones, no TV, but it does have indoor plumbing!

Jan Shore

Skill level: Intermediate
Block size sewn into quilt: 12" x 12"
Number of blocks: 10
Finished quilt size: 88" x 97"

SUPPLIES

Note: Yardage is based on 42" wide cotton fabric.
- 1/8 yd. of mottled black
- 1/4 yd. of medium sage green tonal
- 1/4 yd. of red tonal
- 1/4 yd. of rust tonal
- 1/3 yd. of medium green print
- 3/4 yd. of lavender tonal
- 3/4 yd. of medium blue tonal
- 1 yd. of light green print
- 1-1/4 yds. of mottled dark teal
- 1-1/4 yds. of gold print
- 1-1/2 yds. of light blue tonal
- 1-1/2 yds. of pale green print
- 3-1/4 yds. of mottled cream
- 96" x 105" piece of backing fabric
- 96" x 105" piece of batting
- 5 yds. of 18" wide fusible web
- 1 yd. of white medium-weight fusible interfacing
- Thread in colors to match fabrics
- Rotary cutter, ruler, and mat
- Black fine-point permanent marker
- Template plastic
- Basic sewing and pressing supplies

CUTTING INSTRUCTIONS

From the rust tonal, cut:
One 3-1/2" x 9-1/2" strip (for steps)

From the lavender tonal, cut:
One 4-1/2" x 42" strip; recut into twenty-eight
   1-1/2" x 4-1/2" pieces
Two 3-1/2" x 42" strips
Two 1-1/2" x 42" strips (for strip set)

From the medium blue tonal, cut:
Five 4-1/2" x 42" strips

From the light green print, cut:
Ten 2-1/4" x 42" strips (for binding)

From the mottled dark teal, cut:
Six 4-1/2" x 42" strips
One 2-1/2" x 42" strip (for strip set)

From the gold print, cut:
Four 9-1/2" x 42" strips

From the light blue tonal, cut:
Six 4-1/2" x 42" strips; recut into fifty-three
   4-1/2" squares

From the pale green print, cut:
Two 20" x 42" strips (for hill)
Two 3-1/2" x 42" strips (for foreground)

From the mottled cream, cut:
Two 11" x 42" strips (for sky)
Nine 6-1/2" x 42" strips (for border)
Two 3-1/2" x 34" strips (for fence)

INSTRUCTIONS

Note: Use a 1/4" seam allowance throughout. Press seams toward the darker fabric after adding each piece or as indicated. Trace the patterns for pieces A and B onto template plastic and cut out neatly.

Star Block Section Assembly

1. Following **Diagram 1**, position the piece A template on the 4-1/2" x 42" medium blue tonal strips. Cut 66 A pieces. Position the piece B template on the 4-1/2" x 42" mottled dark teal strips and cut 66 B pieces and 66 B pieces in reverse (Br).

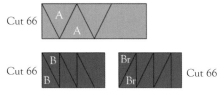

Diagram 1

2. Sew the 2-1/2" x 42" mottled dark teal strip lengthwise between the two 1-1/2" x 42" lavender tonal strips as shown in **Diagram 2**. Crosscut fourteen 2-1/2" wide segments. Stitch a 1-1/2" x 4-1/2" lavender tonal piece to the top of each segment and another one to the bottom to complete ten block centers and four sashing squares. Press seams toward the lavender pieces.

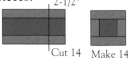

Diagram 2

3. Sew a piece B to one angled side of a piece A and a piece Br to the other side (see **Diagram 3**). Press seams toward the B and Br pieces. Make a total of 66 A/B units.

Make 66
Diagram 3

4. Referring to the **Block Diagrams** and noting orientation, stitch an A/B unit to each of two opposite sides of a block center. Press seams toward the block center. Sew an A/B unit between two 4-1/2" light blue tonal squares. Repeat to make a second section, then stitch these sections to the top and bottom of the block center section. Press seams toward the top and bottom sections. Make a total of ten blocks.

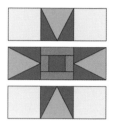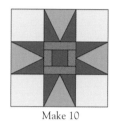

Make 10

Block Diagrams

5. Following **Diagram 4** and noting orientation, sew a 4-1/2" light blue tonal square between two A/B units. Press seams toward the light blue square. Make a total of 13 sashing units.

Make 13
Diagram 4

6. Referring to **Diagram 5**, stitch five blocks alternately together with four sashing units. Press seams toward the blocks. Repeat to make a second row. Sew five sashing units alternately together with four sashing squares. Stitch the sashing row between the block rows to complete the 28-1/2" x 76-1/2" star block section. Press seams toward the sashing row.

Diagram 5

51

Scenic Section Assembly

1. Sew the two 20" x 42" pale green print strips short ends together to make one long strip. Trim to measure 76-1/2" long. Repeat for the 3-1/2" x 42" pale green strips and the 11" x 42" mottled cream strips.

2. Measure and use the marker to mark lines approximately 3/4" apart on the two 3-1/2" x 34" mottled cream strips for the fence. Mark four lines on the 3-1/2" x 9-1/2" rust tonal strip for the steps.

3. Referring to **Diagram 6**, stitch the rust tonal strip between the two 3-1/2" x 34" mottled cream strips. Sew the 3-1/2" x 76-1/2" pale green strip to the bottom and the 20" x 76-1/2" pale green strip to the top. Press seams toward the pale green strips. Stitch the 11" x 76-1/2" mottled cream strip to the top to complete the 36-1/2" x 76-1/2" scenic section. Press seams open.

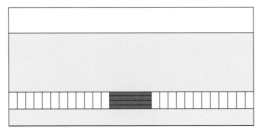

Diagram 6

Appliqué

1. Cut two 8-1/2" x 18" strips from the fusible web. Remove the paper backing. Following manufacturer's directions, fuse onto the wrong side of the remaining lavender tonal fabric. Cut two 4" x 31" strips from the fused fabric. Draw a line down the center of each strip on the paper side as shown in **Diagram 7**. Freehand draw a curve approximately 2" to 2-1/2" wide across the middle of each strip, making sure to keep the center line within the curve area. Cut out the curves. Remove the paper backing. Referring to the **Quilt Layout Diagram** for placement, position a curve over the seam between the cream and green strips on the scenic section. (**Note:** There will be a gap between the curve strips in the center of the seam. This will be covered by the middle house.) Fuse in place.

center line

Diagram 7

2. Cut two 17" pieces from the fusible interfacing. Following manufacturer's instructions, fuse onto the wrong side of the remaining mottled cream fabric. Cut two 17" x 18" pieces from the fusible web. Remove the paper backing and fuse onto the interfacing side of the interfaced fabric. Cut one 15" x 22" piece and one 9" x 16" piece from the fused fabric for the houses.

3. Cut two 1-1/2" x 18" strips from the fusible web. Remove the paper backing, then fuse onto the wrong side of the red tonal fabric. Cut one 1" x 9" piece for the middle house door, two 1" x 6" pieces for the left house door and right house door, two 1" x 3" pieces for middle house chimneys, and two 1" x 2" pieces for right house chimneys.

4. Cut one 1-1/2" x 18" strip from the fusible web. Remove the paper backing, then fuse onto the wrong side of the remaining mottled dark teal fabric. Cut thirteen 1" squares for windows.

5. Using the patterns provided, trace the indicated number of appliqué shapes onto the paper side of the fusible web, leaving at least 1/2" between shapes. Cut out roughly. Fuse the shapes onto the wrong side of the fabrics designated on the patterns. Cut out neatly. Set aside the flowers and leaves for the border. Referring to the **Quilt Layout Diagram** for placement, remove the paper backing and arrange the shapes on the scenic section. Fuse in place. Stitch all shapes in place using matching thread.

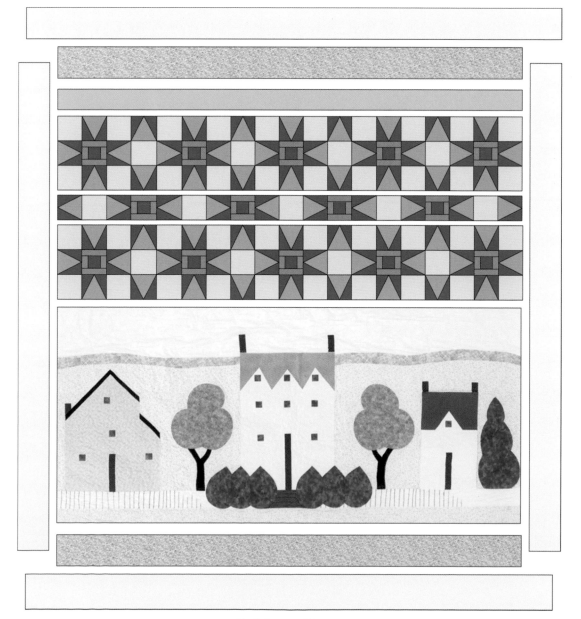

Quilt Layout Diagram

Quilt Assembly and Finishing

1. Referring to the **Quilt Layout Diagram**, sew the star block section to the top of the scenic section. Press seam toward the star block section.

2. Stitch the two 3-1/2" x 42" lavender tonal strips short ends together to make one long strip. Trim to measure 76-1/2" long. Sew the four 9-1/2" x 42" gold print strips short ends together to make one long strip. Press seams to one side. Cut two 76-1/2" lengths. Stitch the lavender strip to the top of the star block section. Press seam toward the strip. Sew a gold strip to the top of the lavender strip and the other gold strip to the bottom of the scenic section to complete the 76-1/2" x 85-1/2" quilt center. Press seams toward the gold strips.

3. *Border*. Stitch the nine 6-1/2" x 42" mottled cream strips short ends together to make one long strip. Press seams to one side. Cut two 85-1/2" lengths and two 88-1/2" lengths. Sew the shorter strips to the sides of the quilt center and the longer strips to the top and bottom. Press seams toward the border.

4. Referring to the **Quilt Layout Diagram** for placement, remove the paper backing and arrange the flowers and leaves on the border. Fuse in place. Stitch all shapes in place using matching thread.

5. Layer the quilt top right side up on top of the batting and the wrong side of the backing. Quilt as desired. Trim backing and batting even with the quilt top.

6. Bind as desired using the ten 2-1/4" x 42" light green print strips.

Jim Shore's hand drawing of quilt. ©JSHORE

Designed by Kathy Atwell • **Pieced by Pine Tree Country Quilts** • **Finished quilt size:** 88" x 97"

Follow the Star

One of the advantages I have as an artist is that my creative drive isn't bogged down with a lot of training. I never went to art school, never had to abide by the rules. Consequently I use color in a way that most trained artists would find unconventional. I'm not afraid to put a pink next to an orange next to a purple next to a green, as long as it works. But sometimes simple is best. And with all the variations and combinations I use, my favorite color is still just plain blue. In my mind, it's the best color to tell this most important story.

Jim Shore

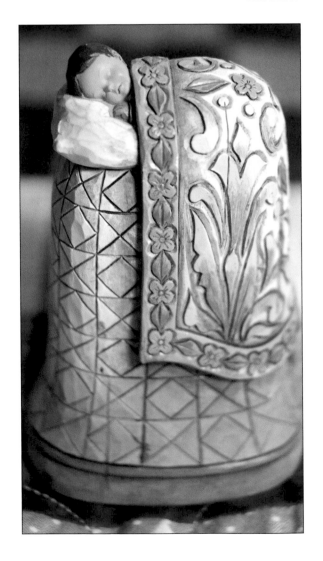

I love, love, *love* this quilt. I love the star-within-a-star pattern. And I really love the message this quilt represents. The blues and whites in this quilt make it all happen for me. Blue is my favorite color, so this quilt has it all. Also, the nativity is simply lovely.

Jan Shore

Skill level: Intermediate
Block size sewn into quilt: 9" x 9", 9" x 9", 18" x 18"
Number of blocks: 8, 7, 18
Finished quilt size: 96" x 114"

SUPPLIES

Note: Yardage is based on 42" wide cotton fabric.
• 1-3/4 yds. of mottled medium blue
• 2-3/4 yds. of mottled dark blue
• 4-1/2 yds. of light blue tonal
• 4-3/4 yds. of solid white
• 104" x 122" piece of backing fabric
• 104" x 122" piece of batting
• Thread in colors to match fabrics
• Rotary cutter, ruler, and mat
• Template plastic
• Basic sewing supplies

CUTTING INSTRUCTIONS

From the mottled medium blue, cut:
One 6-1/2" x 42" strip; recut into four 6-1/2" squares
Four 4-3/4" x 42" strips; recut into thirty 4-3/4" squares

From the mottled dark blue, cut:
Five 3-1/2" x 42" strips (for strip sets)
One 3-1/2" x 42" strip; recut into eight 3-1/2" squares
Ten 3-1/2" x 42" strips (for sixth border)
Eleven 2-1/4" x 42" strips (for binding)
Four 2" x 42" strips (for first border)

From the light blue tonal, cut:
Eleven 5-3/8" x 42" strips; recut into seventy-two 5-3/8" squares, then cut diagonally in half *once*
Two 3-1/2" x 42" strips (for pieces B and Br)
Four 3-1/2" x 42" strips (for strip sets)
Ten 3-1/2" x 42" strips (for second and fourth borders)

From the solid white, cut:
Three 7-1/4" x 42" strips; recut into thirteen 7-1/4" squares, then cut diagonally in half *twice*

Eleven 5-3/8" x 42" strips; recut into seventy-two 5-3/8" squares, then cut diagonally in half *once*
One 3-7/8" x 42" strip; recut into eight 3-7/8" squares, then cut diagonally in half *once*
Two 3-1/2" x 42" strips (for piece A)
Three 3-1/2" x 42" strips; recut into thirty-two 3-1/2" squares

INSTRUCTIONS

Note: Use a 1/4" seam allowance throughout. Press seams toward the darker fabric after adding each piece or as indicated.

Cutting Pieces A to Cr

1. Trace the patterns provided onto template plastic. Cut out neatly and label.

2. Unfold the solid white A strips and press flat. Layer the strips right side up. Position the A template as shown in **Diagram 1** on the layered strips and cut 32 A pieces (16 from each strip). In the same manner, but this time placing the layered strips wrong sides together to cut one piece B and one piece Br with each cut, cut 32 B pieces and 32 Br (reverse) pieces from the light blue tonal B strips.

3. In the same manner, cut 72 piece C and 72 piece Cr (reverse) pieces from the remaining solid white fabric, 72 piece C from the remaining mottled medium blue fabric, and 72 piece Cr from the remaining light blue tonal fabric.

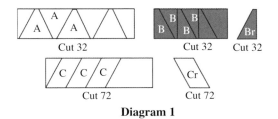

Diagram 1

Sun Rays Block Assembly

1. Referring to the **Sun Rays Block Diagrams**, sew a light blue piece B to one angled side of a white piece A and a light blue piece Br to the other angled side. Make a total of 32 units.

2. Stitch four units together with one 3-1/2" mottled dark blue square and four 3-1/2" solid white squares to make one 9-1/2" x 9-1/2" block. Press seams toward the block center section. Make a total of eight blocks.

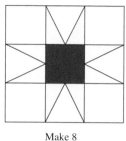

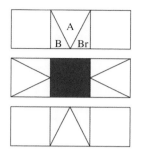

Make 8

Sun Rays Block Diagrams

Nine-Patch Block Assembly

1. Following **Diagram 2** and using 3-1/2" x 42" strips, sew a light blue tonal strip lengthwise between two mottled dark blue strips. Repeat to make a second strip set. Crosscut fourteen 3-1/2" wide segments (A). Stitch a mottled dark blue strip lengthwise between two light blue tonal strips, then crosscut seven 3-1/2" wide segments (B).

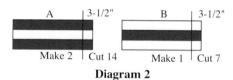

Diagram 2

2. Referring to the **Nine-Patch Block Diagram**, sew a B segment between two A segments to make one 9-1/2" x 9-1/2" block. Press seams away from the center segment. Make a total of seven blocks.

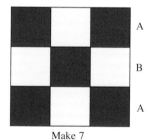

Make 7

Nine-Patch Block Diagram

Hunter's Star Block Assembly

1. Following **Diagram 3**, sew a mottled medium blue piece C to one short side of a 5-3/8" solid white triangle and a light blue tonal piece Cr to the other short side. Press seams toward the triangle. Stitch a 5-3/8" solid white triangle to the top. Press seam toward the triangle. Make a total of 72 dark units.

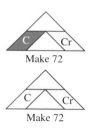

Make 72

Make 72

Diagram 3

2. In the same manner as for step 1, use solid white C and Cr pieces with 5-3/8" light blue tonal triangles to make 72 light units.

3. Referring to the **Hunter's Star Block Diagrams**, sew a light unit to a dark unit. Make a total of four units. Stitch the units together to make one 18-1/2" x 18-1/2" block. Make a total of 18 blocks.

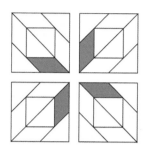

Make 18

Hunter's Star Block Diagrams

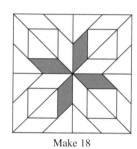

59

Quilt Assembly and Finishing

1. Referring to the **Quilt Layout Diagram**, sew the Sun Rays blocks and Nine-Patch blocks alternately together into five horizontal rows of three blocks each. Stitch the rows together to complete the 27-1/2" x 45-1/2" quilt center.

2. *First border.* Sew the four 2" x 42" mottled dark blue strips short ends together to make one long strip. Press seams to one side. Cut two 45-1/2" lengths and two 30-1/2" lengths. Stitch the longer strips to the long sides of the quilt center and the shorter strips to the top and bottom. Press seams toward the strips.

3. *Second border.* Sew the ten 3-1/2" x 42" light blue tonal strips short ends together to make one long strip. Press seams to one side. Cut two 48-1/2" lengths, two 36-1/2" lengths, two 66-1/2" lengths, and two 54-1/2" lengths. Stitch the 3-1/2" x 48-1/2" strips to the long sides of the quilt top and the 3-1/2" x 36-1/2" strips to the top and bottom. Press seams toward the strips.

4. *Third border units.* Following **Diagram 4** and noting orientation, sew a 7-1/4" solid white triangle to each of two opposite sides of a 4-3/4" mottled medium blue square. Make a total of 22 side units. Stitch a 7-1/4" solid white triangle to one side of a 4-3/4" mottled medium blue square and a 3-7/8" solid white triangle to each of two more sides. Make a total of eight corner units. Sew seven side units together as shown in **Diagram 5**, then stitch a corner unit to each end to make one side strip. Press seams in one direction. Repeat to make a second strip. Sew four side units together, then stitch a corner unit to each end. Repeat to make a second strip. Sew a 6-1/2" mottled medium blue square to each end of these strips to complete the top and bottom strips.

5. *Third (pieced) border.* Stitch a side pieced strip to each long side of the quilt top. Sew the remaining pieced strips to the top and bottom. Press seams toward the second border.

6. *Fourth border.* Stitch the 3-1/2" x 66-1/2" light blue tonal strips to the long sides of the quilt top and

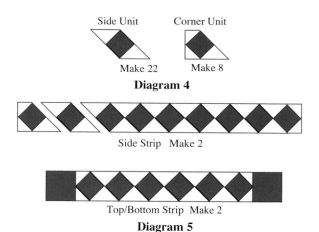

Side Unit   Corner Unit

Make 22   Make 8

Diagram 4

Side Strip   Make 2

Top/Bottom Strip   Make 2

Diagram 5

the 3-1/2" x 54-1/2" light blue tonal strips to the top and bottom. Press seams toward the strips.

7. *Fifth (pieced) border*. Sew four Hunter's Star blocks together. Repeat to make a second strip, then stitch to the long sides of the quilt top. Sew five Hunter's Star blocks together. Repeat to make a second strip, then stitch to the top and bottom of the quilt top. Press seams toward the fourth border.

8. *Sixth border*. Sew the ten 3-1/2" x 42" mottled dark blue strips short ends together to make one long strip. Press seams to one side. Cut two 108-1/2" lengths and two 96-1/2" lengths. Stitch the longer strips to the long sides of the quilt top and the shorter strips to the top and bottom. Press seams toward the strips.

9. Layer the quilt top right side up on top of the batting and the wrong side of the backing. Quilt as desired. Trim backing and batting even with the quilt top.

10. Bind as desired using the eleven 2-1/4" x 42" mottled dark blue strips.

Quilt Layout Diagram

Jim Shore's hand drawing of quilt. ©JSHORE

Designed by Jan Shore • **Pieced by Iva Mintz** • **Finished quilt size:** 96" x 114"

Give Thanks

It's not an exaggeration to say that cornucopias are old-fashioned. They date back to ancient Greece and have been a sign of abundance and blessing for literally thousands of years. As a symbol of harvest, they have a special meaning to me. My grandmother would keep fresh-baked cookies in an old recycled tin with a cornucopia on the side. I think it originally contained fruit of some sort but I didn't care. Reaping a handful of my grandmother's cookies was infinitely sweeter. Needless to say, cornucopias are a recurring theme in my art.

Jim Shore

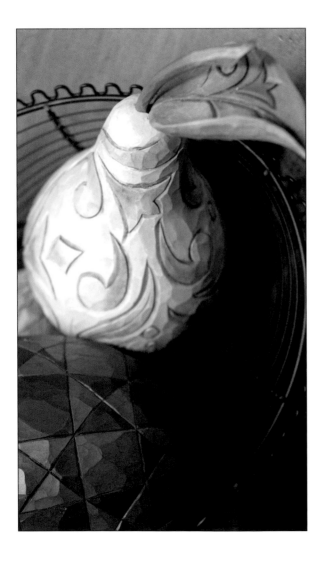

Skill level: Beginner/Intermediate
Finished quilt size: 24" x 36"

SUPPLIES

Note: Yardage is based on 42" wide cotton fabric
- Scraps of light, medium, and dark greens; olive green; lavender; medium and dark reds; light and dark yellows; medium and dark pinks; dark orange; brown; and three different purples
- 1/8 yd. of pale gold tonal
- One fat quarter of orange print
- 1/4 yd. of gold print
- 1/4 yd. of red dot
- 5/8 yd. of mottled cream
- 5/8 yd. of mottled yellow
- 30" x 42" piece of backing fabric
- 30" x 42" piece of batting
- 2 yds. of 18" wide fusible web
- 5/8 yd. of white medium-weight fusible interfacing
- Thread in colors to match fabrics
- Rotary cutter, ruler, and mat
- Basic sewing and pressing supplies

When I designed this wall hanging, I tried to be really faithful to Jim's cornucopia. It has such a great flow to it. The piece is so intricate — it turned out beautiful! If you like appliqué, this one's for you.

Jan Shore

CUTTING INSTRUCTIONS

From the red dot, cut:
Three 1-1/2" x 42" strips (for inner border)

From the mottled cream, cut:
One 18-1/2" x 30-1/2" piece

From the mottled yellow, cut:
Three 2-1/2" x 42" strips (for outer border)

INSTRUCTIONS

Note: Use a 1/4" seam allowance throughout. Press seams toward the darker fabric after adding each piece or as indicated.

1. *Inner border.* Sew the three 1-1/2" x 42" red dot strips short ends together to make one long strip. Cut two 18-1/2" lengths and two 32-1/2" lengths. Stitch the shorter strips to the short sides of the 18-1/2" x 30-1/2" mottled cream piece. Sew the longer strips to the long sides. Press seams away from the quilt center.

2. *Outer border.* Stitch the three 2-1/2" x 42" mottled yellow strips short ends together to make one long strip. Cut two 20-1/2" lengths and two 36-1/2" lengths. Sew the shorter strips to the short sides of the quilt top and the longer strips to the long sides. Press seams away from the quilt center.

3. *Appliqués.* Following manufacturer's directions, apply fusible interfacing to the wrong side of the gold tonal and gold print fabrics. Prepare a full-size template of the cornucopia pattern. (**Note:** The pattern is provided in reverse for fusible appliqué.) Trace the indicated number of shapes onto the paper side of the fusible web, leaving at least 1/2" between shapes. Transfer the piece numbers onto the fusible web to aid in placement. Cut out roughly. Following manufacturer's directions, fuse the shapes onto the wrong side of the fabrics designated on the patterns. Cut out neatly.

Place the full-size template on a bright window or light box and trace the pattern onto the other side of the paper to prepare a placement pattern. Place the pattern right side up on your ironing board, then place the quilt top over the pattern so the motif is in the middle of the quilt center. Remove the paper backing and arrange the shapes on the quilt center, using the pattern as a guide and working from the back to the front. Fuse in place. Stitch all shapes in place using matching thread.

4. Layer the quilt top right side up on top of the batting and the wrong side of the backing. Quilt as desired. Trim backing and batting even with the quilt top.

5. Bind as desired using the four 2-1/4" x 42" mottled yellow strips.

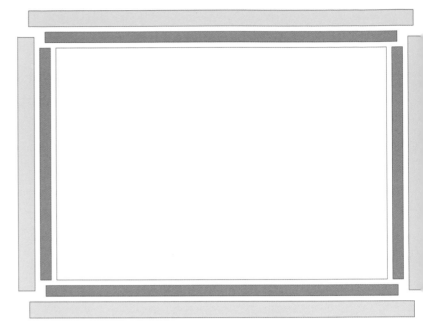

Quilt Layout Diagram

Jim Shore's hand drawing of quilt. ©JSHORE

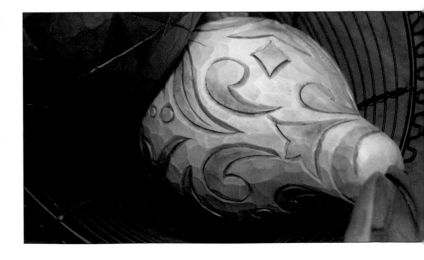

Designed by Jan Shore • Pieced by Pine Tree Country Quilts • Finished quilt size: 24" x 36"

The Sky's the Limit

I'm afraid of heights. I don't like flying and get no thrill out of being on top of the Empire State Building or Sears Tower. The only time I've ever enjoyed being higher up than a step ladder was in a hot air balloon. Maybe it was the silence. Maybe the fact I could actually understand the physical properties holding me up. (I am after all an engineer.) But it was a great experience, full of contrast and color. From the bright shapes of the balloon to the deep blue of the sky to the green on green patterning of the fields below, it was a sight permanently etched in my mind.

Jim Shore

Skill level: Intermediate
Finished quilt size: 48-7/8" x 48-7/8"

SUPPLIES

Note: Yardage is based on 42" wide cotton fabric.
- 1/4 yd. of aqua/white print
- 1/3 yd. of aqua paisley
- 1/3 yd. of aqua tonal
- 1/3 yd. of mottled blue
- 1/2 yd. of light green tonal
- 5/8 yd. of yellow tonal
- 2/3 yd. of mottled lavender
- 7/8 yd. of red dot
- 1-1/8 yds. of white tonal
- 57" x 57" piece of batting
- 57" x 57" piece of batting
- Thread in colors to match fabrics
- Rotary cutter, ruler, and mat
- Basic sewing supplies

CUTTING INSTRUCTIONS

From the aqua/white print, cut:
Two 2-1/2" x 42" strips (for strip sets)

From the aqua paisley, cut:
Three 2-1/2" x 42" strips (for strip sets)

From the aqua tonal, cut:
Three 2-1/2" x 42" strips (for strip sets)

From the mottled blue, cut:
One 8-3/4" x 42" strip; recut into two 8-3/4" squares, then cut diagonally in half *once*

From the light green tonal, cut:
One 12" x 42" strip; recut into two 12" squares, then cut diagonally in half *once*

From the yellow tonal, cut:
Five 3-1/2" x 42" strips (for border)

From the mottled lavender, cut:
One 8-1/2" x 42" strip; recut into one 8-1/2" square and four 3-1/2" squares
Four 2-1/2" x 28-3/4" strips

From the red dot, cut:
Two 3-1/2" x 28-3/4" strips
Two 3-1/2" x 22-3/4" strips
Five 2-1/4" x 42" strips (for binding)

From the white tonal, cut:
One 6-1/2" x 42" strip; recut into six 6-1/2" squares, then cut two squares diagonally in half *once*
One 4-1/8" x 42" strip; recut into one 4-1/8" square, then cut diagonally in half *twice*
Two 2-7/8" x 42" strips; recut into twenty 2-7/8" squares, then cut diagonally in half *once*
Eight 2-1/2" x 42" strips (for strip sets)

INSTRUCTIONS

Note: Use a 1/4" seam allowance throughout. Press seams toward the darker fabric after adding each piece or as indicated.

I've always wanted to ride in a hot air balloon, but I have to admit I am a chicken. These balloons are really sweet. This quilt reminds me of how I think the ride would be, as you rise toward the sky things get smaller and smaller. Maybe one day...

Jan Shore

69

Center Medallion Assembly

1. Following **Diagram 1**, sew a 6-1/2" white tonal triangle to each side of the 8-1/2" mottled lavender square. Stitch a 8-3/4" mottled blue triangle to each side of this unit, then a 12" light green tonal triangle.

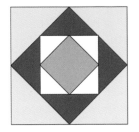

Diagram 1

2. Sew a 3-1/2" x 22-3/4" red dot strip to each of two opposite sides of the center unit and a 3-1/2" x 28-3/4" red dot strip to the remaining sides.

3. Draw a diagonal line on the wrong side of each of the four 6-1/2" white tonal squares. Place a marked square right sides together on each corner of the center unit as shown in **Diagram 2**. Stitch on the drawn lines, trim seam allowance to 1/4", and press the triangles open.

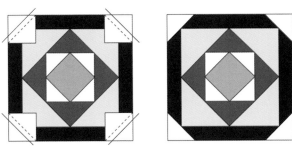

Diagram 2

4. Referring to **Diagram 3**, sew a 2-1/2" x 28-3/4" mottled lavender strip to each of two opposite sides of the center unit. Stitch a 4-1/8" white tonal triangle to each end of the remaining mottled lavender strips, then sew to the other sides to complete the 32-3/4" x 32-3/4" center medallion.

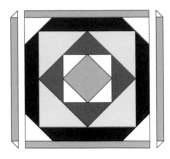

Diagram 3

Checkerboard Corner Section Assembly

1. Following **Diagram 4** and using 2-1/2" x 42" strips, sew an aqua tonal strip lengthwise to a white tonal strip. Make a total of three strip sets. Crosscut forty-four 2-1/2" wide segments (A). In the same manner, stitch an aqua/white print strip to a white tonal strip. Make a total of two strip sets, then crosscut 20 segments (B). Sew an aqua paisley strip to a white tonal strip. Make a total of three sets, then crosscut 36 segments (C).

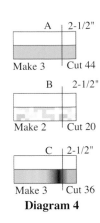

Diagram 4

2. Stitch the segments together as shown in **Diagram 5** to make a total of four of each row. Remove the white square from the end of each odd-numbered row. Sew a 2-7/8" white tonal triangle to the right end of each row (see **Diagram 6**). Referring to **Diagram 7**, stitch the rows together, then sew a 2-7/8" white tonal triangle to the bottom of each section to complete four checkerboard corner sections.

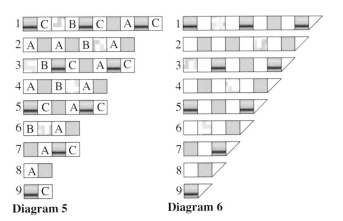

Diagram 5   **Diagram 6**

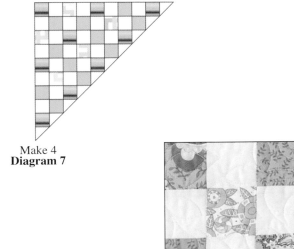

Make 4
Diagram 7

Quilt Assembly and Finishing

1. Referring to the **Quilt Layout Diagram**, sew a checkerboard corner section to each side of the center medallion to complete the 43-3/8" x 43-3/8" quilt center. Press seams toward the center medallion.

2. *Border*. Stitch the five 3-1/2" x 42" yellow tonal strips short ends together to make one long strip. Press seams to one side. Cut four 43-3/8" lengths. Sew a strip to each of two opposite sides of the quilt center. Stitch a 3-1/2" mottled lavender square to each end of the remaining strips, then sew to the other sides. Press seams toward the strips.

3. Layer the quilt top right side up on top of the batting and the wrong side of the backing. Quilt as desired. Trim backing and batting even with the quilt top.

4. Bind as desired using the five 2-1/4" x 42" red dot strips.

Quilt Layout Diagram

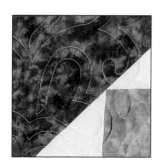

71

Jim Shore's hand drawing of quilt. ©JSHORE

Designed by Kathy Atwell • **Pieced by Pine Tree Country Quilts** • **Finished quilt size:** 48-7/8" x 48-7/8"

The Simple Life

Growing up in the country, you learn to be self-sufficient. You have to be your own mechanic, carpenter, welder, or 'Jack' of whatever other trade that needs to be done. Sometimes you love the work, sometimes not. But it never goes away and there's always something else to do. Your livestock and your livelihood depend on it. It's really great training for an artist, keeping the mind and body active. And when you do get a quiet moment, you find yourself surrounded by the simple beauty of the land.

Jim Shore

Wouldn't everyone love to live on this farm! This takes me back to the home of my grandparents, with the big red barn and mules in the fields. The colors in this table runner are so bold. You will really have fun with this project. I love the blend of the old and new.

Jan Shore

Skill level: Intermediate
Finished runner size: 22" x 74"
Finished placemat size: 12" x 16"

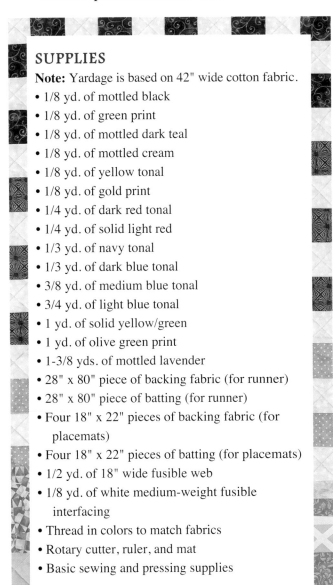

SUPPLIES

Note: Yardage is based on 42" wide cotton fabric.

- 1/8 yd. of mottled black
- 1/8 yd. of green print
- 1/8 yd. of mottled dark teal
- 1/8 yd. of mottled cream
- 1/8 yd. of yellow tonal
- 1/8 yd. of gold print
- 1/4 yd. of dark red tonal
- 1/4 yd. of solid light red
- 1/3 yd. of navy tonal
- 1/3 yd. of dark blue tonal
- 3/8 yd. of medium blue tonal
- 3/4 yd. of light blue tonal
- 1 yd. of solid yellow/green
- 1 yd. of olive green print
- 1-3/8 yds. of mottled lavender
- 28" x 80" piece of backing fabric (for runner)
- 28" x 80" piece of batting (for runner)
- Four 18" x 22" pieces of backing fabric (for placemats)
- Four 18" x 22" pieces of batting (for placemats)
- 1/2 yd. of 18" wide fusible web
- 1/8 yd. of white medium-weight fusible interfacing
- Thread in colors to match fabrics
- Rotary cutter, ruler, and mat
- Basic sewing and pressing supplies

CUTTING INSTRUCTIONS

From the mottled dark teal, cut:
One 2-1/2" x 42" strip; recut into four 2-1/2" squares

From the yellow tonal, cut:
One 2-1/2" x 42" strip (for strip set)

From the gold print, cut:
One 2-1/2" x 42" strip (for strip set)

From the dark red tonal, cut:
One 2-1/2" x 42" strip (for strip set)
One 1-1/4" x 42" strip; recut into six 1-1/4" squares

From the solid light red, cut:
One 2-1/2" x 42" strip (for strip set)
One 1-1/4" x 42" strip; recut into four 1-1/4" squares

From the navy tonal, cut:
Three 2-1/2" x 42" strips; cut each strip in half (for strip sets)

From the dark blue tonal, cut:
Three 2-1/2" x 42" strips; cut each strip in half (for strip sets), then recut one half-strip into six 2-1/2" squares

From the medium blue tonal, cut:
Three 2-1/2" x 42" strips (for strip sets)
One 2-1/2" x 42" strip; recut into four 2-1/2" squares and two 1-3/4" squares

From the light blue tonal, cut:
Five 2-1/2" x 42" strips; cut each strip in half (for strip sets)
Three 2-1/2" x 42" strips (for strip sets)
One 2-1/2" x 42" strip; recut into ten 2-1/2" squares and two 1-3/4" squares

From the solid yellow/green, cut:
Two 2-1/2" x 42" strips (for runner strip sets)
Fifteen 1-1/2" x 42" strips (for placemats)

From the olive green print, cut:
Two 2-1/2" x 42" strips (for runner strip sets)
Fifteen 1-1/2" x 42" strips (for placemats)

From the mottled lavender, cut:
Seven 3-1/4" x 42" strips (for placemat binding)
Five 2-1/4" x 42" strips (for runner binding)
One 1-3/4" x 42" strip; recut into two 1-3/4" squares, four 1-1/2" x 31/2" pieces, and two 1-1/2" x 2-1/2" pieces
Five 1-1/2" x 42" strips (for border)

INSTRUCTIONS

Note: Use a 1/4" seam allowance throughout. Press seams toward the darker fabric after adding each piece or as indicated.

Checkerboard Section Assembly

   1. Following **Diagram 1** and using 2-1/2" x 21" strips, sew three navy tonal strips alternately with two light blue tonal strips to make a U strip set. Repeat with three light blue tonal strips and two navy tonal strips to make a V strip set. Crosscut eight 2-1/2" wide U segments and eight 2-1/2" wide V segments.

In the same manner, use three dark blue tonal strips and two light blue tonal strips to make a W strip set, and three light blue tonal strips and two dark blue tonal strips to make an X strip set. Crosscut eight 2-1/2" wide W segments and eight 2-1/2" wide X segments.

Stitch a 2-1/2" x 42" medium blue tonal strip to a 2-1/2" x 42" light blue tonal strip. Make a total of three strip sets. Crosscut thirty-four 2-1/2" wide segments (Y) and six 1-1/2" wide segments (Z).

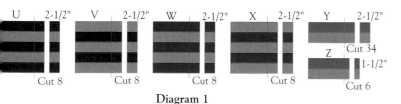

Diagram 1

2. Sew a U segment short ends together with a V segment as shown in **Diagram 2** to make one row. Make a total of eight rows. Stitch the rows together to complete the navy section.

3. Referring to **Diagram 3**, sew a W segment short ends together with an X segment to make one row. Make a total of six rows. Stitch three rows together to complete one dark blue section. Repeat to make a second section. Following the **Checkerboard Diagram**, sew the dark blue sections to the sides of the navy section.

Make 8
Diagram 2

Make 6
Diagram 3

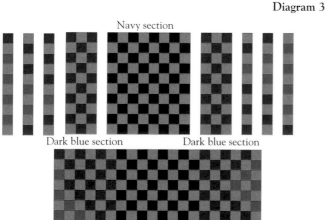

Checkerboard Diagram

4. Stitch a W segment and a Y segment together with two 2-1/2" light blue tonal squares and one 2-1/2" dark blue tonal square to make one row (see **Diagram 4**). Repeat to make a second row. Sew to the sides of the pieced section.

5. Referring to **Diagram 5**, stitch an X segment together with two Y segments and one 2-1/2" dark blue tonal square to make one row. Repeat to make a second row. Sew to the sides of the pieced section.

6. Stitch four Y segments together with one 2-1/2" dark blue tonal square and one 2-1/2" light blue tonal square as shown in **Diagram 6** to make one row. Repeat to make a second row. Sew to the sides of the pieced section to complete the 20-1/2" x 40-1/2" checkerboard section.

Make 2
Diagram 4

Make 2
Diagram 5

Make 2
Diagram 6

Scenic Section Assembly

1. Following **Diagram 7** and using 2-1/2" x 42" strips, sew the dark red tonal strip to the solid light red strip. Crosscut twelve 2-1/2" wide segments and eight 1-1/2" wide segments. Stitch the yellow tonal strip to the gold print strip, then crosscut

eight 2-1/2" wide segments and two 1-1/2" wide segments. Sew a solid yellow/green strip to an olive green print strip. Repeat to make another strip set, then crosscut twenty-six 2-1/2" wide segments and four 1-1/2" wide segments.

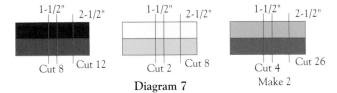

Diagram 7

2. Trim the yellow/green edge of each of four 2-1/2" green segments to measure 1-1/4" wide as shown in **Diagram 8**. Trim the olive green edge of each of two 2-1/2" green segments to measure 1-1/4" wide and the olive green edge of the 1-1/2" green segments to measure 1-1/4" wide.

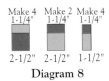

Diagram 8

3. Draw a diagonal line on the wrong side of the 1-1/4" dark red tonal and solid light red squares; 1-3/4" light blue tonal, medium blue tonal, and mottled lavender squares; and the 2-1/2" mottled dark teal squares. Referring to **Diagram 9**, place a marked 1-1/4" solid light red square right sides together on one corner of a 2-1/2" light blue tonal square. Stitch on the drawn line, trim seam allowance to 1/4", and press the triangle open. Repeat to make a second unit. Repeat with 1-1/4" dark red tonal squares and 2-1/2" medium blue tonal squares to make four medium blue units, a 1-3/4" medium blue tonal square on a dark red tonal corner and a 1-3/4" light blue tonal square on a solid light red corner of two red segments to make two red units, a 1-1/4" solid light red square on a light blue corner of two Y segments to make two Y units, and a 1-1/4" dark red tonal square on one medium blue corner of two Z segments to make two Z units.

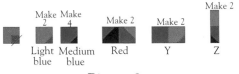

Diagram 9

4. Sew a Y segment together with a Z segment, 1-1/2" x 3-1/2" mottled lavender piece, 1-1/2" green segment, and a trimmed 2-1/2" green segment to make Section A (see **Diagram 10**). Repeat to make a second section.

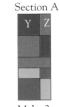

Section A

Make 2
Diagram 10

5. Following **Diagram 11**, stitch three 2-1/2" red segments together with two 1-1/2" red segments. Place a marked 1-3/4" mottled lavender square right sides together on one corner of the section, sew on the drawn line, trim seam allowance to 1/4", and press the triangle open to complete one Section B. Repeat to make a second section.

Section B

Make 2
Diagram 11

6. Stitch a 1-1/2" x 3-1/2" mottled lavender piece together with a trimmed 1-1/2" green segment and a trimmed 2-1/2" green segment as shown in **Diagram 12** to make one Section C. Repeat to make a second section.

Section C

Make 2
Diagram 12

7. Sew two 2-1/2" red segments together with two 1-1/2" red segments, two Y segments, and one Z unit to make one Section D (see **Diagram 13**). Repeat to make a second section.

Section D

Make 2
Diagram 13

8. Following **Diagram 14**, stitch a Y unit together with a red unit, medium blue unit, and a Y segment to make one Section E. Repeat to make a second section.

Section E

Make 2
Diagram 14

9. Sew four 2-1/2" yellow segments and one 1-1/2" yellow segment together as shown in **Diagram 15**. Place a mottled dark teal square right sides together on one top corner, stitch on the drawn line, trim seam allowance to 1/4", and press the triangle open. Repeat on the remaining top corner. Sew a Z segment to the teal end of the unit to complete one Section F. Repeat to make a second section.

Section F

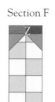

Make 2
Diagram 15

10. Stitch a Y segment, trimmed 2-1/2" green segment, 1-1/2" x 2-1/2" mottled lavender piece, and a 2-1/2" light blue tonal square together to make one Section G (see **Diagram 16**). Repeat to make a second section.

Section G

Make 2
Diagram 16

11. Following **Diagram 17**, sew four Y segments together with one light blue unit and one medium blue unit to make one Section H. Repeat to make a second section.

Section H

Make 2
Diagram 17

12. Stitch ten 2-1/2" green segments together to make one Lawn Section as shown in **Diagram 18**. Repeat to make a second section.

Lawn Section

Make 2
Diagram 18

13. Referring to **Diagram 19**, sew one of each section together to complete one 16-1/2" x 20-1/2" scenic section. Repeat to make a second section.

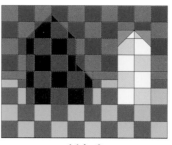

Make 2
Diagram 19

Appliqué

1. Cut one 1" x 10" strip from the fusible web. Following manufacturer's directions, fuse onto the wrong side of the remaining dark red tonal fabric. Cut two 1/2" x 3" pieces for doors and two 1/2" x 1" pieces for chimneys.

2. Cut one 1" x 6" strip from the fusible web. Fuse onto the wrong side of the mottled black fabric. Cut two 1/2" x 3/4" pieces for house windows and four 1/2" x 1" pieces for barn windows.

3. Cut one 4" x 5" piece from the fusible interfacing. Fuse onto the wrong side of the mottled cream fabric.

4. Using the patterns provided, trace the indicated number of appliqué shapes onto the paper side of the fusible web, leaving at least 1/2" between shapes. Cut out roughly. Following manufacturer's directions, fuse the shapes onto the wrong side of the fabrics designated on the patterns. Fuse the fences onto the interfaced section of the mottled cream fabric. Cut out neatly. Referring to the photo for placement, remove the paper backing and arrange the shapes on the scenic sections. Fuse in place. Stitch all shapes in place using matching thread.

Runner Assembly and Finishing

1. Referring to the **Runner Center Diagram**, sew the scenic sections to the top and bottom of the checkerboard section to complete the 20-1/2" x 72-1/2" runner center.

2. *Border*. Stitch the five 1-1/2" x 42" mottled lavender strips short ends together to make one long strip. Press seams to one side. Cut two 72-1/2" lengths and two 22-1/2" lengths. Sew the longer strips to the long sides of the runner and the shorter strips to the top and bottom.

3. Layer the runner top right side up on top of the runner batting and the wrong side of the runner backing. Quilt as desired. Trim backing and batting even with the runner top.

4. Bind as desired using the five 2-1/4" x 42" mottled lavender strips.

Placemat Assembly and Finishing

1. Following **Diagram 20** and using 1-1/2" x 42" strips, sew eight olive green print strips alternately together with seven solid yellow/green strips. Crosscut twenty-four 1-1/2" wide segments (L). In the same manner, stitch eight solid yellow/green strips to seven olive green strips, then crosscut twenty 1-1/2" wide segments (M).

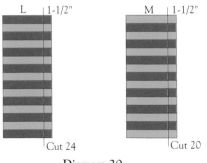

Diagram 20

Runner Center Diagram

2. Referring to the **Placemat Layout Diagram**, sew six L segments together with five M segments to complete one placemat top. Make a total of four tops.

3. Layer each placemat top right side up on top of a piece of placemat batting and the wrong side of a piece of placemat backing. Quilt as desired. Trim backing and batting even with the placemat top.

4. Bind as desired using the seven 3-1/4" x 42" mottled lavender strips, stitching the binding to the placemats using a 1/2" seam allowance.

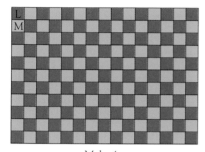

Make 4
Placemat Layout Diagram

Jim Shore's hand drawing of placemat. ©JSHORE

Jim Shore's hand drawing of runner. ©JSHORE

Designed by Jim and Jan Shore • Pieced by Pine Tree Country Quilts • Finished runner size: 22" x 74"

Finished placemat size: 12" x 16"

Stars and Stripes Forever

Over the course of the years, I've designed over 3,000 different Santa Clauses. Because of that, people think I'm some sort of Christmas nut—waiting all year for that one special day. Don't get me wrong—I do love Christmas. And I love to draw Santas (they all look a little bit like me). But my favorite holiday is the fourth of July. There's nothing better than a summer evening with Carolina barbecue and fireworks. And I can't pass up a chance to celebrate the freedoms we enjoy and the courage of those who fought for them.

Jim Shore

Skill level: Intermediate
Finished quilt size: 45" x 48"

SUPPLIES

Note: Yardage is based on 42" wide cotton fabric.

- 1/3 yd. of mottled navy
- 1/3 yd. of mottled light blue
- 1/3 yd. of mottled lavender
- 1/2 yd. of medium blue print
- 2/3 yd. of gold tonal
- 1-3/8 yds. of red tonal
- 1-2/3 yds. of mottled cream
- 53" x 56" piece of backing fabric
- 53" x 56" piece of batting
- 3 yds. of 18" wide fusible web
- Thread in colors to match fabrics
- Rotary cutter, ruler, and mat
- Template plastic
- Basic sewing and pressing supplies

This wall hanging is truly amazing. And the figurines that inspired it are pretty amazing too. Jim and I are both very patriotic, so this piece was a natural. The painting of George Washington is an original Jim Shore oil painting and is hanging in the dining room at Kilburnie.

Jan Shore

CUTTING INSTRUCTIONS

From the mottled navy, cut:
Three 2-1/2" x 42" strips; recut into twenty-five
    2-1/2" squares and ten 2-1/2" x 4-1/2" pieces

From the mottled light blue, cut:
Two 2-1/2" x 42" strips (for strip sets)
One 2-1/2" x 42" strip; recut into two 2-1/2" squares
    and one 2-1/2" x 4-1/2" piece

From the mottled lavender, cut:
Two 1-1/2" x 41-1/2" strips (for border)
Three 1-1/2" x 42" strips (for border)

From the medium blue print, cut:
One 2-1/2" x 42" strip (for strip set)
Four 2-1/2" x 42" strips; recut into thirty-four 2-1/2"
    squares and fifteen 2-1/2" x 4-1/2" pieces

From the gold tonal, cut:
Five 2-1/4" x 42" strips (for binding)
Five 1-1/2" x 42" strips (for border)

From the red tonal, cut:
Five 9" x 42" strips; recut into one 9" x 15" strip,
    one 9" x 22" strip, one 9" x 24" strip, one 9" x 25"
    strip, one 9" x 39" strip, and one 9" x 42" strip

From the mottled cream, cut:
One 16-1/2" x 42" strip; recut into one 16-1/2" x
    21-1/2" piece and one 8-1/2" x 13-1/2" piece
One 8-1/2" x 41-1/2" strip
One 8-1/2" x 33-1/2" strip
One 4-1/2" x 42" strip; recut into six 4-1/2" squares
    and one 4-1/2" x 9-1/2" piece
Three 2-1/2" x 42" strips (for strip sets)
Four 2-1/2" x 42" strips; recut into fifty-six 2-1/2"
    squares and four 2-1/2" x 4-1/2" pieces

INSTRUCTIONS

Note: Use a 1/4" seam allowance throughout. Press
seams toward the darker fabric after adding each
piece or as indicated.

Star Unit Assembly

1. Draw a diagonal line on the wrong side of each
of the 2-1/2" mottled cream squares, twelve 2-1/2"
mottled navy squares, and sixteen 2-1/2" medium

blue print squares. Following **Diagram 1**, place a
marked mottled cream square right sides together on
each end of a 2-1/2" x 4-1/2" mottled navy piece.
Sew on the drawn lines, trim seam allowance to 1/4",
and press triangles open. Make a total of ten side
units. Repeat with mottled cream squares and
medium blue print pieces to make fifteen side units,
mottled cream squares and mottled light blue pieces
to make one side unit, mottled navy squares and a
mottled cream piece to make one side unit, and
medium blue print squares and a mottled cream piece
to make one side unit.

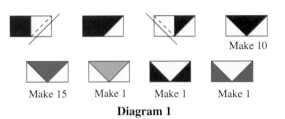

Make 10

Make 15   Make 1   Make 1   Make 1

Diagram 1

2. Place a marked 2-1/2" mottled navy square on
each corner of a 4-1/2" mottled cream square as
shown in **Diagram 2**. Stitch on the drawn lines, trim
1/4" beyond the lines, and press the triangles open.
Repeat to make two center units. In the same manner,

make one center unit using two 2-1/2" mottled navy squares and two 2-1/2" medium blue print squares on a 4-1/2" mottled cream square. Make three center units using 2-1/2" medium blue print squares on a 4-1/2" mottled cream square.

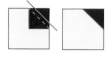

Make 2 Make 1 Make 3

Diagram 2

3. Place a marked 2-1/2" mottled cream square right sides together with a 2-1/2" mottled navy square (see **Diagram 3**). Stitch on the drawn line, trim seam allowance to 1/4", then press the cream triangle open. In the same manner, make a total of three units using 2-1/2" medium blue print squares and 2-1/2" mottled cream squares.

Make 1   Make 3

Diagram 3

4. Referring to **Diagram 4** and noting orientation, sew the side units, center units, and 2-1/2" squares together to make one of each unit shown.

  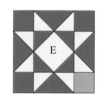

A   B   C   D   E   F

G   H

Diagram 4

Checkerboard Section Assembly

1. Following **Diagram 5** and using 2-1/2" x 42" strips, sew a mottled cream strip lengthwise to a mottled light blue strip. Repeat to make a second strip set. Crosscut twenty-four 2-1/2" wide segments. In the same manner, stitch a mottled cream strip to a medium blue print strip and crosscut ten 2-1/2" wide segments.

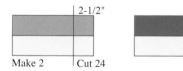

2-1/2"   2-1/2"

Make 2   Cut 24   Cut 10

Diagram 5

2. Referring to **Diagram 6**, sew four cream/medium blue segments together to make section I, four cream/light blue segments together for section J, two cream/medium blue segments and two cream/light blue segments together for section K, seven cream/light blue segments and one 2-1/2" x 4-1/2" mottled cream piece together for section L, one cream/medium blue segment and seven cream/light blue segments together for section M, one cream/medium blue segment and four cream/light blue segments together for section N, and one cream/medium blue segment and one 2-1/2" x 4-1/2" mottled cream piece together for section O.

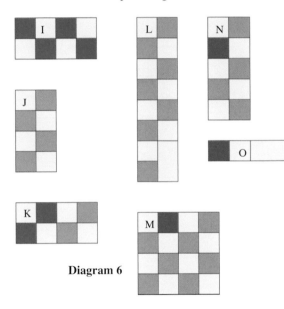

Diagram 6

Quilt Center Assembly

1. Referring to the **Quilt Layout Diagram**, sew the 4-1/2" x 9-1/2" mottled cream piece to the I section. Press seam toward the cream pieces throughout this step. Stitch the 8-1/2" x 13-1/2" mottled cream piece to the J section. Sew the two pieced sections together.

2. Stitch the K section to the E unit. Sew this section to the section made in step 1 (main section). Stitch the L section to the 16-1/2" x 21-1/2" mottled cream piece, then sew this to the main section. Stitch the G unit, C unit, D unit, and M section together. Sew to the main section. Stitch the 8-1/2" x 33-1/2" mottled cream strip to the bottom of the main section.

3. Sew the A unit, B unit, and F unit together. Stitch a cream/medium blue segment to one end of the H unit, then add the N and O sections. Sew this to the bottom of the A/B/F section, then stitch to the main section.

4. Sew the 8-1/2" x 41-1/2" mottled cream strip to the bottom of the main section to complete the 41-1/2" x 44-1/2" quilt center.

Appliqué

1. Cut the following 8" wide strips from the fusible web: 14", 21", 23", 24", 38", and 41".

2. Use the pattern provided to draw a curve onto template plastic and cut out neatly. Use the template to trace one hump curve on the paper side of the 14" fusible web strip. Trace one hump curve, then turn the template and trace a valley curve on the 21" fusible web strip as shown in **Diagram 7**. In the same manner, trace one hump and one valley on the 23" fusible web strip; one hump, one valley, and one hump on the 24" fusible web strip; one hump, one valley, one hump, one valley on the 38" fusible web strip; and one hump, one valley, one hump, one valley, and one hump on the 41" fusible web strip. Roughly cut out the curves.

Diagram 7

3. Turn the quilt center wrong side up. Following **Diagram 8**, place the 14" curve on the top of the quilt center with the beginning of the curve 2" down from the top edge. Mark the edges of the squares onto the fusible web that the red stripe will butt against. Mark along the top edge of the quilt center. Remove the paper backing and fuse the marked strip onto the wrong side of the 15" red strip. Cut out neatly.

4. Repeat step 3 for all fusible web and red tonal strips to make six stripes. Referring to the **Quilt Layout Diagram** for placement, arrange the stripes on the right side of the quilt center, positioning the first stripe 2" down from the top and leaving 4" between stripes. Fuse in place. Stitch all stripes in place using matching thread.

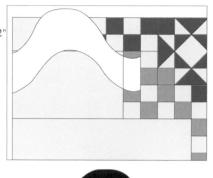

Diagram 8

Quilt Layout Diagram

Jim Shore's hand drawing of quilt. ©JSHORE

Quilt Finishing and Assembly

1. *Inner border.* Sew the 1-1/2" x 41-1/2" mottled lavender strips to the top and bottom of the quilt center. Press seams toward the border. Stitch the three 1-1/2" x 42" mottled lavender strips short ends together to make one long strip. Press seams to one side. Cut two 46-1/2" lengths, then sew to the sides of the quilt center. Press seams toward the border.

2. *Outer border.* Stitch the five 1-1/2" x 42" gold tonal strips short ends together to make one long strip. Press seams to one side. Cut two 43-1/2" lengths and two 48-1/2" lengths. Sew the shorter strips to the top and bottom of the quilt top and the longer strips to the sides. Press seams away from the quilt center.

3. Layer the quilt top right side up on top of the batting and the wrong side of the backing. Quilt as desired. Trim backing and batting even with the quilt top.

4. Bind as desired using the five 2-1/4" x 42" gold tonal strips.

Designed by Jim and Jan Shore • Pieced by Pine Tree Country Quilts • Finished quilt size: 45" x 48"

Backgammon

Kids today have it a lot worse than we did in a lot of ways. One of the most basic is in the games they play. We had games with simple rules and certain outcomes, played on works of art with stark, contrasting colors and precise geometric design. There are not many things more beautiful in the world than the simple checkerboard, or more whimsical than the crooked paths of Parcheesi. Kids today miss that simple design in games. Plus it's hard to throw your 36" HD plasma screen TV at your older brother when he cheats.

Jim Shore

Skill level: Intermediate
Finished quilt size: 80" x 88"

SUPPLIES

Note: Yardage is based on 42" wide cotton fabric.
- 3/4 yd. of green tonal
- 1-1/2 yds. of mottled lavender
- 2-3/4 yds. of mottled cream
- 3-1/8 yds. of mottled red
- 6-1/4 yds. of solid black
- 88" x 96" piece of batting
- 88" x 96" piece of batting
- Thread in colors to match fabrics
- 12 yds. of 18" wide fusible web
- 7 yds. of 1/4" fusible web tape
- 1/4" bias bar
- Rotary cutter, ruler, and mat
- Long straight edge or yardstick
- Template plastic
- Basic sewing and pressing supplies

The backgammon and chess set that Jim has made is fabulous. My suggestion to you is to make great big backgammon pieces (mine look like pancakes) and big dice with yoyo's for the dots (21 for each of the dice). Take this quilt out to the yard and teach someone how to play while you're having a picnic.

Jan Shore

93

CUTTING INSTRUCTIONS

From the green tonal, cut:
One 18" x 42" strip (for bias stems)

From the mottled lavender, cut:
Eight 2-1/2" x 42" strips (for border)
Nine 2-1/4" x 42" strips (for binding)

From each of the mottled cream and mottled red, cut:
Twelve 7-1/2" x 32-1/2" strips

From the solid black, cut:
Eleven 7-1/2" x 64" *lengthwise* strips
Two 4-1/2" x 64" *lengthwise* strips
Two 6-1/2" x 84-1/2" *lengthwise* strips

INSTRUCTIONS

Note: Use a 1/4" seam allowance throughout. Press seams toward the darker fabric after adding each piece or as indicated.

Quilt Center Assembly

1. Following **Diagram 1** and using 7-1/2" x 32-1/2" strips, sew six mottled red strips alternately together with six mottled cream strips. Repeat to make a second strip set. Stitch the strip sets lengthwise together, alternating colors, to complete the background. Sew a 6-1/2" x 84-1/2" solid black strip to

Diagram 1

each long side of the unit to complete the background. Press seams toward the strips.

2. Cut eleven 6" x 74" strips and two 4" x 64" strips from the fusible web. Center and fuse a strip onto the wrong side of the 7-1/2" x 64" solid black strips and the 4-1/2" x 64" solid black strips. Fold each 7-1/2" x 64" fused strip lengthwise in half with fused side out and then in half widthwise. Mark 1/8" from the long folded edge on the open ends as shown in **Diagram 2**. Place a straightedge or yardstick from the top of the fusible web at the short folded edge to the mark. Trim along the straightedge. Open the folds to yield one black diamond. Repeat for all 7-1/2" x 64" fused strips.

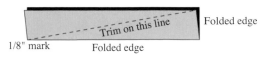

Diagram 2

3. Fold each 4-1/2" x 64" fused strip widthwise in half with fused side out. Mark 1/8" from the long bottom edge (see **Diagram 3**). Trim from the folded edge to the mark. Open the fold to yield one black half-diamond. Repeat for the remaining 4-1/2" x 64" fused strip.

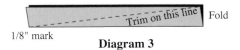

Diagram 3

4. Remove the paper backing from one diamond. Referring to **Diagram 4**, place the narrow pointed ends against the black strips 7-1/4" from the top edge of the background with the center corners aligned with the center seam of the background. Fuse in place. Fuse the remaining diamonds down the length of the background with the outer points 7" from the previously fused diamonds and the center corners just touching. Place a half-diamond on the top edge of the background with the center corner just touching the center corner of the topmost diamond and the pointed ends against the black strips. Fuse in place. Repeat for the bottom edge of the background. Stitch all diamonds and half-diamonds in place using matching thread.

Diagram 4

5. Following **Diagram 5**, trim one end of the 18" x 42" green tonal strip at a 45° angle. Cut 1-1/4" bias strips to equal 250". Sew half of the strips short ends together to make one 125" long strip. Fold the strip lengthwise in half wrong sides together. Stitch along the raw edges using a *scant* 1/4" seam allowance. Trim the seam allowance to 1/8". Flatten the strip with the seam centered on one side. Insert the bias bar into the strip, then press the strip flat to make one vine piece. Repeat with the remaining bias strips to make another vine piece.

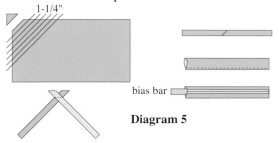

Diagram 5

6. Apply fusible web tape to the seam side of each vine piece. Referring to the photo for placement, arrange the vine pieces on the black strips, staying at least 3/8" away from the edges of the black strips. Trim excess. Fuse in place. Sew along the edges of the vines using matching thread to secure.

Quilt Assembly and Finishing

1. *Border*. Sew the eight 2-1/2" x 42" mottled lavender strips short ends together to make one long strip. Press seams to one side. Cut two 84-1/2" lengths and two 80-1/2" lengths. Stitch the longer strips to the long sides of the quilt center and the shorter strips to the other sides. Press seams toward the strips.

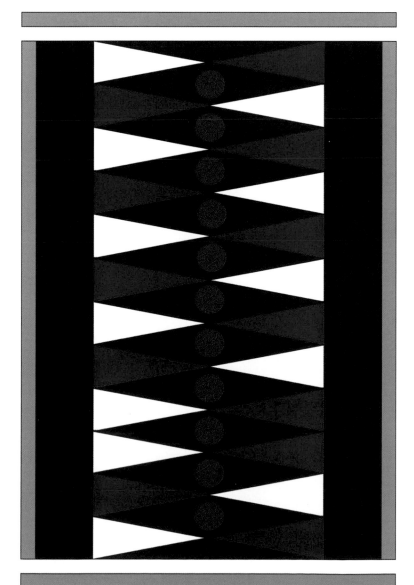

Quilt Layout Diagram

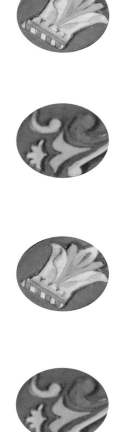

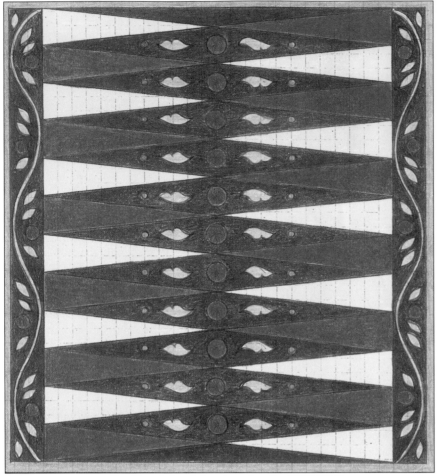

Jim Shore's hand drawing of quilt. ©JSHORE

2. *Appliqué.* Using the patterns provided, trace the indicated number of appliqué shapes onto the paper side of the fusible web, leaving at least 1/2" between shapes. Cut out roughly. Fuse the shapes onto the wrong side of the fabrics designated on the patterns. Cut out neatly. Referring to the photo for placement, arrange the border leaves and red circles on the black strips. Fuse in place. Fuse the center leaves 5-1/2" from the quilt center on the black diamonds, then fuse the lavender small circles 2-1/2" from the leaves. Sew all shapes in place using matching thread.

3. Layer the quilt top right side up on top of the batting and the wrong side of the backing. Quilt as desired. Trim backing and batting even with the quilt top.

4. Bind as desired using the nine 2-1/4" x 42" mottled lavender strips.

5. Trace the yo-yo circle pattern onto template plastic and cut out neatly. Use the template to cut 11 circles from the remaining red tonal fabric. Thread a needle with two strands of red thread and tie a strong knot. Turn the edge of one circle 1/4" to the wrong side while sewing a long running stitch (at least 1/2") around the edge as shown in **Diagram 6**. Pull tightly to gather. Flatten. Repeat for all yo-yo circles. Hand stitch the circles to the center of the black diamonds.

Diagram 6

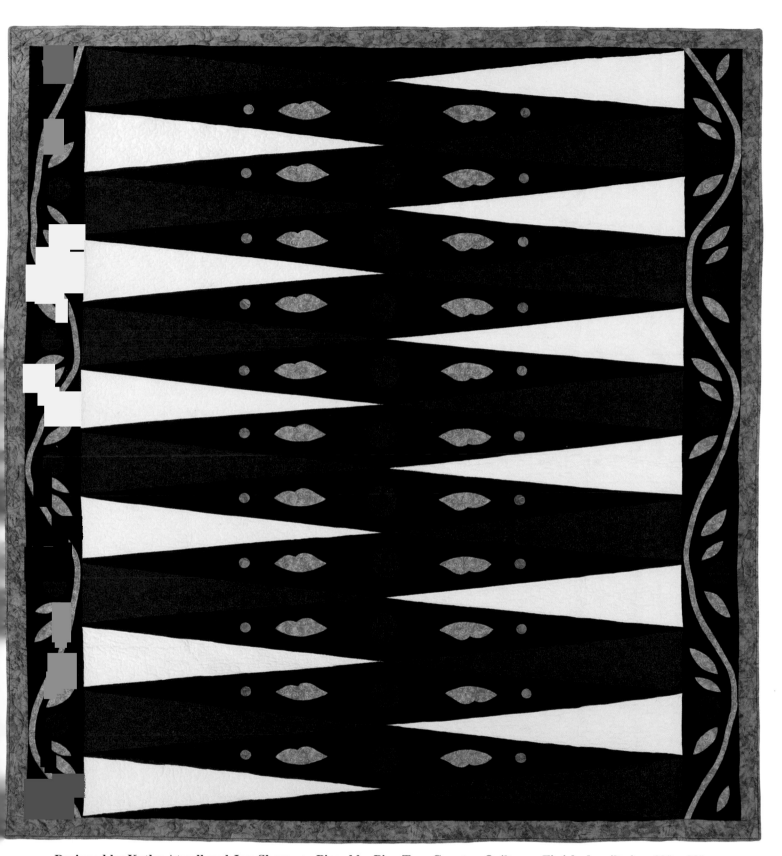

Designed by Kathy Atwell and Jan Shore • **Pieced by Pine Tree Country Quilts** • **Finished quilt size:** 80" x 88"

Frosty Friends

Growing up in South Carolina, we didn't see too many snowstorms. When a good one came through, with real packing snow and temperatures cold enough to keep it around, we were outside playing full bore until our fingers and toes were numb. I loved it, and snowmen and winter scenes have always been a major theme in my art. But the best part was coming inside, wrapped in something warm by the fire. There's nothing more pleasant in the world than being inside, cozy and warm, during a good hard snow.

Jim Shore

Skill level: Beginner
Block size sewn into quilt: 9" x 9"
Number of blocks: 49
Finished quilt size: 75" x 75"

SUPPLIES

Note: Yardage is based on 42" wide cotton fabric.

- 5/8 yd. of lavender tonal
- 5/8 yd. of solid light blue
- 7/8 yd. of light blue print
- 1 yd. of dark blue tonal
- 1-1/2 yds. of purple tonal
- 2-1/2 yds. of solid cream
- 83" x 83" piece of backing fabric
- 83" x 83" piece of batting
- Thread in colors to match fabrics
- Rotary cutter, ruler, and mat
- Template plastic
- Basic sewing supplies

While this quilt is made of stars, it really has the look of snowflakes. I don't know if its just the choice of colors or if I'm being fanciful. I love the figure of the snowman and the little boy. Although it kind of makes me sad: our son Michael will be a senior upon returning to school. Why do they all insist on growing up way too fast!

Jan Shore

CUTTING INSTRUCTIONS

From the lavender tonal, cut:
Five 3-1/2" x 42" strips (for strip sets)

From the solid light blue, cut:
Five 3-1/2" x 42" strips (for strip sets)

From the light blue print, cut:
Seven 3-1/2" x 42" strips (for pieces B and Br)

From the dark blue tonal, cut:
Eight 3-1/2" x 42" strips (for border)

From the purple tonal, cut:
Eight 3-1/2" x 42" strips (for strip sets)
Eight 2-1/4" x 42" strips (for binding)

From the solid cream, cut:
Eleven 3-1/2" x 42" strips; recut into one hundred
    twenty-five 3-1/2" squares
Eight 3-1/2" x 42" strips (for strip sets)
Five 3-1/2" x 42" strips (for piece A)

INSTRUCTIONS

Note: Use a 1/4" seam allowance throughout. Press seams toward the darker fabric after adding each piece or as indicated.

Nine-Patch Block Assembly

1. Following **Diagram 1** and using 3-1/2" x 42" strips, sew a solid cream strip lengthwise between two lavender tonal strips. Repeat to make a second strip set, then crosscut twenty-four 3-1/2" wide segments (lavender A). Stitch a lavender tonal strip between two solid cream strips, then crosscut twelve 3-1/2" wide segments (lavender B). Sew a solid cream strip between two solid light blue strips. Repeat to make a second strip set, then crosscut twenty-four 3-1/2" wide segments (light blue A). Stitch a solid light blue strip between two solid cream strips, then crosscut twelve 3-1/2" wide segments (light blue B).

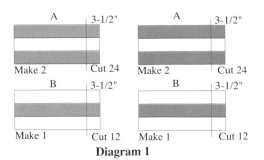

Diagram 1

2. Referring to the **Nine-Patch Block Diagrams,** sew a lavender B segment between two lavender A segments to make one 9-1/2" x 9-1/2" lavender block. Make a total of 12 blocks. In the same manner, use light blue segments to make a total of 12 light blue blocks.

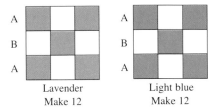

Nine-Patch Block Diagrams

Sun Rays Block Assembly

1. Trace the patterns provided for pieces A and B onto template plastic. Cut out neatly and label. Use the templates to cut 100 A pieces from the 3-1/2" x 42" solid cream strips and 100 B pieces from the 3-1/2" x 42" light blue print strips. Reverse the B template and cut 100 Br pieces from the 3-1/2" x 42" light blue print strips.

2. Following **Diagram 2**, sew a piece B to one angled side of a piece A, then stitch a piece Br to the other angled side. Make a total of 100 sar point units.

Diagram 2

3. Referring to the **Sun Rays Block Diagram**, sew four star point units together with five 3-1/2" solid cream squares into horizontal rows. Press seams toward the units. Stitch the rows together to complete one 9-1/2" x 9-1/2" block. Press seams toward the center section. Make a total of 25 blocks.

Make 25
Sun Rays Block Diagram

Quilt Assembly and Finishing

1. Referring to the **Quilt Layout Diagram** and noting color placement, sew the Nine-Patch blocks alternately together with the Sun Rays blocks into seven horizontal rows of seven blocks each. Stitch the rows together to complete the 63-1/2" x 63-1/2" quilt center.

2. *Pieced border*. Following **Diagram 3** and using 3-1/2" x 42" strips, sew a dark blue tonal strip lengthwise to a purple tonal strip. Make a total of eight strip sets, then crosscut ninety-two 3-1/2" wide segments. Referring to the **Quilt Layout Diagram**, stitch 21 segments together, alternating colors. Repeat to make a second strip, then sew to opposite sides of the quilt center. Press seams toward the border. Stitch 25 segments together in the same manner, then repeat to make a second strip. Sew these strips to the other sides of the quilt center. Press seams toward the border.

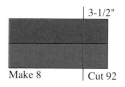

3-1/2"

Make 8 | Cut 92
Diagram 3

3. Layer the quilt top right side up on top of the batting and the wrong side of the backing. Quilt as desired. Trim backing and batting even with the quilt top.

4. Bind as desired using the eight 2-1/4" x 42" purple tonal strips.

Quilt Layout Diagram

Jim Shore's hand drawing of quilt. ©JSHORE

Designed by Jan Shore • **Pieced by Sue Weisberger** • **Finished quilt size:** 75" x 75"

Love Blooms Here

I don't know many artists who don't love gardening. There's an obvious appeal in color and shape, the natural beauty of life. And to me there's always been something else, an appreciation of the process of growth, the nurturing needed and the time it takes for a seed to become a flower. There's an urgency about it, you can't waste a day. It reminds me of something my father used to say when he was trying to teach me more about life through gardening: "The best time to plant a tree is 25 years ago—or right now!"

Jim Shore

Skill level: Intermediate
Finished quilt size: 48" x 54"

SUPPLIES

Note: Yardage is based on 42" wide cotton fabric.

- Scraps of tonals in pink, red, terra cotta, and yellow
- Scrap of red/orange print
- One fat quarter (18" x 22") of mottled tan
- One fat quarter of golden brown tonal
- 1/4 yd. of dark green print
- 1/4 yd. of medium green print
- 1/2 yd. of mottled lavender
- 5/8 yd. of olive green print
- 3/4 yd. of light green print
- 1 yd. of mottled cream
- 1 yd. of blue swirl
- 1-1/4 yds. of sage green tonal
- 56" x 62" piece of backing fabric
- 56" x 62" piece of *Fairfield* Nature-Fil Bamboo batting
- 3-1/2 yds. of 18" wide fusible web
- 2 yds. of white medium-weight fusible interfacing
- Thread in colors to match fabrics
- Appliqué pressing sheet
- Chalk pencil
- Rotary cutter, ruler, and mat
- Basic sewing and pressing supplies

The appliqué here is wonderful. This scene is on the angel and just worked out perfectly for this piece. Jim loves to use purple and here the purple makes the whole scene pop! The quilt is hanging on the back porch of Kilburnie. If you ever come to South Caealacky (South Carolina), go by for a visit. You will fall in love!

Jan Shore

105

CUTTING INSTRUCTIONS

From the mottled lavender, cut:
Two 2-1/2" x 40-1/2" strips (for inner side border)
Two 2-1/2" x 36-1/2" strips (for inner top and
   bottom border)

From the olive green print, cut:
One 8-1/2" x 32-1/2" strip (for back hill)

From the light green print, cut:
One 4-1/2" x 32-1/2" strip (for grass)

From the blue swirl, cut:
One 10" x 32-1/2" strip (for sky)
Eight 2-1/2" x 42" strips (for strip sets)

From the sage green tonal, cut:
Ten 2-1/2" x 42" strips (for strip sets)
Six 2-1/4" x 42" strips (for binding)

INSTRUCTIONS

Note: Use a 1/4" seam allowance throughout. Press seams toward the darker fabric after adding each piece or as indicated.

Quilt Center Assembly

Note: Appliqué patterns are provided in reverse for fusible appliqué and do not require a seam allowance. For hand appliqué, make a template from template plastic for each shape and then trace in reverse on the right side of the appropriate fabrics.

1. Cut one 3" x 32-1/2" strip and two 6-1/2" x 32-1/2" strips from the length of the fusible web.

2. Using the pattern provided, trace the curving pattern for the back hill onto the 3" x 32-1/2" fusible web strip and the pattern for the front hill onto one of the 6-1/2" x 32-1/2" fusible web strips, aligning the top of the curve with one long edge of the fusible web strip. Trace the cloud pattern onto the remaining 6-1/2" x 32-1/2" fusible web strip. Following **Diagram 1**, trim excess fusible web below the marked pattern lines, leaving approximately 1" extending below the lines.

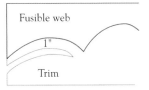

Diagram 1

3. Following manufacturer's directions, apply fusible interfacing to the wrong side of the mottled cream, mottled tan, and remaining light green print fabric. Cut one 15" x 32-1/2" piece from the interfaced mottled cream fabric for the cloud and one 17-3/4" x 32-1/2" piece from the interfaced light green print fabric for the front hill.

4. Remove the paper backing from the front hill fusible web pattern, then position on the wrong side of the interfaced light green print piece, with the top edge of the pattern aligned with one long edge of the fabric. Following manufacturer's directions, fuse in place. Cut out the top of the hill on the drawn line to complete the front hill.

5. Remove the paper backing from the back hill fusible web pattern, then position on the wrong side of the 8-1/2" x 32-1/2" olive green print strip, with the top edge of the pattern aligned with one long edge of the fabric. Fuse in place. Cut out on the drawn line to complete the back hill.

6. Remove the paper backing from the cloud fusible web pattern, then position on the wrong side of the 15" x 32-1/2" interfaced mottled cream piece, with the top edge of the pattern aligned with one long edge of the fabric. Fuse in place. Cut out on the drawn line to complete the cloud.

7. Trace the indicated number of the remaining appliqué shapes onto the paper side of the fusible web, leaving at least 1/2" between shapes. Cut out roughly. Fuse the shapes onto the wrong side of the fabrics designated on the patterns. Cut out neatly.

8. Position the top of the cloud on the bottom of the 10" x 32-1/2" blue swirl strip, with the lowest point of the cloud 1" above the bottom edge of the strip. Mark along the top of the cloud with a chalk pencil. Trim excess fabric at the bottom of the sky strip, leaving 1" below the drawn line as shown in **Diagram 2**. Place the pressing sheet on your ironing board. Remove the paper backing from the cloud, re-align it with the marked line on the sky strip and align the outer edges. Fuse in place.

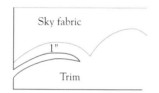

Diagram 2

Quilt Layout Diagram

9. Remove the paper backing from the back hill and the mountain. Position the back hill on the bottom of the cloud, with the outer edges aligned and approximately 1" of the cloud extending below the lowest curve on the hill. Arrange the mountain between the back hill and the front hill. Fuse the pieces in place on the cloud.

10. Remove the paper backing from the front hill. Position on the bottom of the back hill, with outer edges aligned and the back hill extending approximately 1" below the lowest curve of the front hill. Fuse in place.

11. Center and fuse the interfaced tan path onto the 4-1/2" x 32-1/2" light green print strip. Fuse in place. Sew the strip to the bottom of the front hill to complete the quilt center. Press seam toward the strip.

12. Referring to the photo, arrange and fuse the remaining appliqué shapes onto the quilt center, working from back to front and positioning the bottom of the fence and the large shrubs along the seam line between the grass and front hill.

13. Stitch all shapes in place using matching thread.

14. Trim the quilt center to measure 32-1/2" x 40-1/2", removing excess from the sky end.

Quilt Assembly and Finishing

1. *Inner border*. Sew the 2-1/2" x 40-1/2" mottled lavender strips to the sides of the quilt center. Stitch the 2-1/2" x 36-1/2" strips to the top and bottom. Press seams away from the quilt center.

2. Sew a 2-1/2" x 42" blue swirl strip lengthwise between two 2-1/2" x 42" sage green tonal strips. Make a total of four strip sets. Following **Diagram 3**, crosscut three strips sets into twenty-six 4-1/2" wide segments (A) and the remaining strip set into eight 2-1/2" wide segments (C).

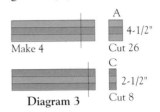

Diagram 3

3. Stitch a 2-1/2" x 42" sage green tonal strip lengthwise between two 2-1/2" x 42" blue swirl strips. Repeat to make a second strip set. Referring to **Diagram 4**, crosscut thirty 2-1/2" wide segments (B).

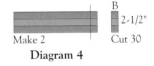

Diagram 4

4. *Outer (pieced) border*. Sew six A segments, seven B segments, and two C segments together as shown in the **Quilt Layout Diagram** to make one side outer border strip. Press seams toward the A and C segments. Repeat to make a second strip, then stitch to the sides of the quilt top. Press seams toward the inner border. Sew seven A segments, eight B segments, and two C segments together to make one strip. Repeat to make a second strip, then stitch the strips to the top and bottom of quilt top.

5. Layer the quilt top right side up on top of the batting and the wrong side of the backing. Quilt as desired. Trim backing and batting even with the quilt top.

6. Bind as desired using the six 2-1/4" x 42" sage green tonal strips.

Jim Shore's hand drawing of quilt. ©JSHORE

Designed by Jim and Jan Shore • **Pieced by Pine Tree Country Quilts** • **Finished quilt size:** 48" x 54"

The Ride of Your Life

Merry-go-rounds and circus acts are an easy source of inspiration. Like most kids in my generation, I grew up on Disney and entertained fantasies of running away to join the circus. Looking back, it's easy to see why that life would appeal to me: the bright colors, raucous crowds, costumes, music, glamour, and of course the allure of show biz. Come to think of it, that life still sounds pretty good!

Jim Shore

The name of this quilt very much describes our lives together. Just like the ride, we've had loads of ups and downs. But through it all, life has been great! This quilt represents our love of family and of all things old. Make sure to grab the brass ring!

Jan Shore

Skill level: Intermediate
Block size sewn into quilt: 8" x 8"
Number of blocks: 20
Finished quilt size: 52" x 52"

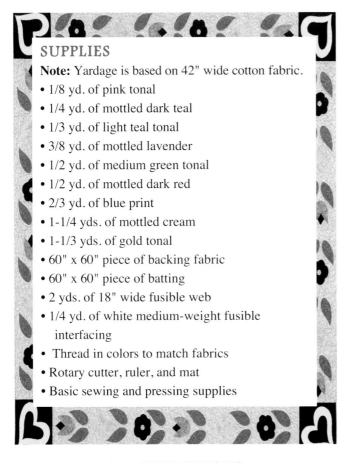

SUPPLIES

Note: Yardage is based on 42" wide cotton fabric.

- 1/8 yd. of pink tonal
- 1/4 yd. of mottled dark teal
- 1/3 yd. of light teal tonal
- 3/8 yd. of mottled lavender
- 1/2 yd. of medium green tonal
- 1/2 yd. of mottled dark red
- 2/3 yd. of blue print
- 1-1/4 yds. of mottled cream
- 1-1/3 yds. of gold tonal
- 60" x 60" piece of backing fabric
- 60" x 60" piece of batting
- 2 yds. of 18" wide fusible web
- 1/4 yd. of white medium-weight fusible interfacing
- Thread in colors to match fabrics
- Rotary cutter, ruler, and mat
- Basic sewing and pressing supplies

CUTTING INSTRUCTIONS

From the mottled dark teal, cut:
Two 2-1/2" x 42" strips (for strip sets)

From the light teal tonal, cut:
Four 2-1/2" x 42" strips (for strip sets)

From the mottled lavender, cut:
Two 2-1/2" x 40-1/2" strips (for sashing)
Reserve remaining fabric for appliqués

From the mottled dark red, cut:
One 6-1/2" x 42" strip; recut into four 6-1/2" squares
Reserve remaining fabric for appliqués

From the blue print, cut:
Two 4-7/8" x 42" strips; recut into twelve 4-7/8" squares, then cut diagonally in half
One 4-1/2" x 42" strip; recut into six 4-1/2" squares

One 3-3/4" x 42" strip; recut into eight 3-3/4" squares, then cut diagonally in half

From the mottled cream, cut:
One 4-7/8" x 42" strip; recut into eight 4-7/8" squares, then cut diagonally in half
One 4-1/2" x 42" strip; recut into four 4-1/2" squares
One 4-1/2" x 40-1/2" strip
One 3-3/4" x 42" strip; recut into twelve 3-3/4" squares, then cut diagonally in half
Six 2-1/2" x 42" strips (for strip sets)

From the gold tonal, cut:
Four 6-1/2" x 40-1/2" strips (for border)
Six 2-1/4" x 42" strips (for binding)

INSTRUCTIONS

Note: Use a 1/4" seam allowance throughout. Press seams toward the darker fabric after adding each piece or as indicated.

Checkerboard Row Assembly

1. Referring to **Diagram 1** and using 2-1/2" x 42" strips, sew the following strips lengthwise together to make the strip sets: mottled dark teal, mottled cream, light teal tonal, mottled cream (A); light teal tonal, mottled cream, mottled dark teal, mottled cream (B); and mottled cream, light teal tonal, mottled cream, light teal tonal (C). Press seams away from the cream strips. Crosscut twelve 2-1/2" wide segments from A, twelve 2-1/2" wide segments from B, and sixteen 2-1/2" wide segments from C.

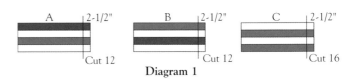

Diagram 1

2. Following **Diagram 2**, stitch the indicated segments together to make a total of ten blocks. Press the seams in the odd-numbered blocks in one direction and the seams in the even-numbered blocks in the opposite direction. Sew the blocks together in the order shown to make two rows. Press seams in one direction.

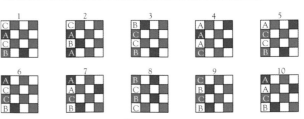

Diagram 2

Square-in-a-Square Row Assembly

1. Sew a 3-3/4" mottled cream triangle to each side of six 4-1/2" blue print squares as shown in the **Square-in-a-Square Block Diagrams**. Press seams toward the triangles. Stitch a 4-7/8" blue print triangle to each side of the units to complete six blue blocks. Press seams toward the blue triangles.

2. Repeat step 1 to make a total of four cream blocks, this time using 4-1/2" mottled cream squares, 4-7/8" mottled cream triangles, and 3-3/4" blue print triangles.

3. Sew three blue blocks alternately together with two cream blocks to make one row. Press seams toward the blue blocks. Repeat to make a second row.

Make 6   Make 4

Square-in-a-Square Block Diagrams

Quilt Assembly and Finishing

1. Referring to the **Quilt Layout Diagram**, sew the checkerboard rows and square-in-a-square rows together with the 4-1/2" x 40-1/2" mottled cream strip and the two 2-1/2" x 40-1/2" mottled lavender strips to complete the 40-1/2" x 40-1/2" quilt center.

Quilt Layout Diagram

2. *Border.* Stitch a 6-1/2" x 40-1/2" gold tonal strip to each of two opposite sides of the quilt center. Press seams away from the quilt center. Sew a 6-1/2" mottled dark red square to each end of the remaining 6-1/2" x 40-1/2" gold tonal strips, then stitch to the other sides. Press seams away from the quilt center.

3. *Appliqués.* Following manufacturer's directions, apply fusible interfacing to the wrong side of the remaining mottled cream fabric. Cut one 2" x 18" strip from the fusible web, then fuse the strip onto the wrong side of the medium green tonal fabric. Cut two 3/8" x 13" strips from the fused fabric for stems. Using the patterns provided, trace the indicated number of appliqué shapes onto the paper side of the fusible web, leaving at least 1/2" between shapes. (**Note:** For reverse pieces, place the templates face down and then trace.) Cut out roughly. Following manufacturer's directions, fuse the shapes onto the wrong side of the fabrics designated on the patterns. Cut out neatly. Referring to the **Quilt Layout Diagram** for placement, remove the paper backing and arrange the shapes on the mottled cream center strip, border, and cornerstones. Fuse in place. Stitch all shapes in place using matching thread.

4. Layer the quilt top right side up on top of the batting and the wrong side of the backing. Quilt as desired. Trim backing and batting even with the quilt top.

5. Bind as desired using the six 2-1/4" x 42" gold tonal strips.

Jim Shore's hand drawing of quilt. ©JSHORE

Designed by Jim Shore and Kathy Atwell • Pieced by Pine Tree Country Quilts • Finished quilt size: 52" x 52"

Winter's Mischief

One of the great things about Christmas at our house is that we're surrounded by family. In fact, with six kids and God knows how many grandkids, sometimes it can be a little too much of a good thing. Don't get me wrong, I'm not complaining, but there's an element of peace, prayerful moments of quiet contemplation, that are an important element of the season. That's why I love Christmas Eve, after the kids have gone to bed and everything's set up for the morning. It's a moment of beauty and promise that I treasure.

Jim Shore

Can you believe that this snowman is throwing snowballs?!? What fun! I love the colors in this quilt, and I really like the way Jim put together the snowman. Just imagine snuggling with this quilt in front of a fire.

Jan Shore

Skill level: Beginner
Block size sewn into quilt: 6" x 6", 3" x 6"
Number of blocks: 63, 32
Finished quilt size: 54" x 66"

SUPPLIES

Note: Yardage is based on 42" wide cotton fabric.
- 7/8 yd. of blue tonal
- 1 yd. of red
- 1-1/8 yds. of aqua
- 1-3/4 yds. of white
- 62" x 74" piece of backing fabric
- 62" x 74" piece of batting
- Thread in colors to match fabrics
- Rotary cutter, ruler, and mat
- Basic sewing supplies

CUTTING INSTRUCTIONS

From the blue tonal, cut:

One 7-1/4" x 42" strip; recut into four 7-1/4" squares, then cut diagonally in half *twice* (discard two triangles)

Four 4-3/4" x 42" strips; recut into two 3-7/8" squares, then cut diagonally in half *once* (for inner border cornerstones); and thirty-two 4-3/4" squares (for block centers)

From the red, cut:

Eight 3-7/8" x 42" strips; recut into eighty 3-7/8" squares, then cut diagonally in half *once* (for block corners)

From the aqua, cut:

Six 3-1/2" x 42" strips (for outer border)
Six 2-1/2" x 42" strips (for binding)

From the white, cut:

One 7-1/4" x 42" strip; recut into five 7-1/4" squares, then cut diagonally in half *twice* (discard two triangles)

Four 4-3/4" x 42" strips; recut into thirty-one 4-3/4" squares (for block centers)

Eight 3-7/8" x 42" strips; recut into eighty 3-7/8" squares, then cut diagonally in half *once* (for block corners and cornerstones)

INSTRUCTIONS

Note: Use a 1/4" seam allowance throughout. Press seams toward the darker fabric after adding each piece or as indicated.

Broken Sash Block Assembly

1. Following **Diagram 1**, sew a 3-7/8" white triangle to one side of a 4-3/4" blue tonal square. Stitch a white triangle to each of the remaining sides as shown in **Diagram 2**.

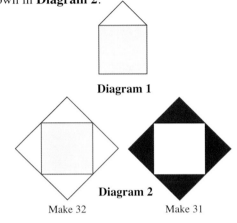

Diagram 1

Diagram 2

Make 32   Make 31

2. Repeat step 1 to make a total of 32 blue/white blocks.

3. In the same manner, use red triangles and white squares to make a total of 31 white/red blocks.

Border Block Assembly

1. Following **Diagram 3**, sew a 3-7/8" white triangle to each short side of a 7-1/4" blue tonal triangle. Trim seams to 1/4" and press open. Make a total of 14 border blocks.

Diagram 3

Make 14

2. In the same manner, use red triangles and 7-1/4" white triangles to make a total of 18 border blocks as shown in **Diagram 4**.

Make 18
Diagram 4

3. *Cornerstones.* Stitch a 3-7/8" blue tonal triangle to a 3-7/8" white triangle (see **Diagram 5**). Make a total of four cornerstones.

Make 4

Diagram 5

Quilt Assembly and Finishing

1. Referring to the **Quilt Layout Diagram**, sew the Broken Sash blocks alternately together into nine horizontal rows of seven blocks each. Stitch the rows together to complete the 42-1/2" x 54-1/2" quilt center.

2. *Inner (pieced) border*. Noting color placement, sew seven border blocks short ends together to make the top border strip. Repeat to make the bottom border strip, then stitch both strips to the quilt center. Sew nine border blocks short ends together to make one side strip, then repeat to make a second strip. Stitch a cornerstone to each end of these pieced strips, then sew to the quilt center.

3. *Outer border*. Stitch the six 3-1/2" x 42" aqua strips short ends together to make one long strip. Cut two 60-1/2" lengths and two 54-1/2" lengths. Sew the longer strips to the sides of the quilt top and the shorter strips to the top and bottom.

4. Layer the quilt top right side up on top of the batting and the wrong side of the backing. Quilt as desired. Trim backing and batting even with the quilt top.

5. Bind as desired using the six 2-1/2" x 42" aqua strips.

Quilt Layout Diagram

149

Jim Shore's hand drawing of quilt. ©JSHORE

Designed by Jan Shore • Pieced by Alison Newman • Finished quilt size: 54" x 66"

Pilgrim Patch

Thanksgiving is a real bonanza for an artist. There's the spiritual aspect that expresses the love and appreciation of God's creation—family, friends, the bounty of the earth, and the magic of being alive. Those are the foundation of all creative thought. Plus there's the physical element as well, with the deep colors of autumn, the reds, purples, and oranges. And great shapes like the horn of a cornucopia or the imperfect roundness of a pumpkin. And then there's the food...

Jim Shore

I really like the idea of using non-traditional colors for different seasons. If there is one thing I have learned from Jim it is to use color and let yourself go with it. No one can accuse Jim of being a traditional colorist!

Jan Shore

Skill level: Intermediate
Block size sewn into quilt: 6" x 6"
Number of blocks: 17
Finished quilt size: 50" x 50"

SUPPLIES

Note: Yardage is based on 42" wide cotton fabric.
- 1/3 yd. of red tonal
- 1/2 yd. of tan tonal
- 1/2 yd. of mottled green
- 1/2 yd. of blue print
- 7/8 yd. of mottled dark cream
- 1-1/8 yds. of stripe
- 1-1/4 yds. of lavender tonal
- 58" x 58" piece of backing fabric
- 58" x 58" piece of batting
- Thread in colors to match fabrics
- Rotary cutter, ruler, and mat
- Template plastic
- Basic sewing supplies

CUTTING INSTRUCTIONS

From the tan tonal, cut:
Two 2-1/2" x 34-1/2" strips (for inner side border)
Two 2-1/2" x 30-1/2" strips (for inner top and
  bottom border)

From the mottled green, cut:
One 4-3/4" x 42" strip; recut into six 3-7/8" squares,
  then cut diagonally in half *once*; and one 4-3/4"
  square
Two 2-1/2" x 42" strips; recut into three 2-1/2" x
  21" strips (for strip sets)

From the blue print, cut:
One 4-1/4" x 42" strip; recut into eight 4-1/4"
  squares, then cut diagonally in half *twice*
One 2-7/8" x 42" strip; recut into twelve 2-7/8"
  squares, then cut diagonally in half *once*
One 2-1/2" x 42" strip; recut into five 2-1/2" squares
One 2-1/2" x 42" strip (for A and B pieces)

From the mottled dark cream, cut:
Two 6-1/2" x 42" strips; recut into twelve 6-1/2"
  squares
One 4-1/4" x 42" strip; recut into eight 4-1/4"
  squares, then cut diagonally in half *twice*
One 2-7/8" x 42" strip; recut into twelve 2-7/8"
  squares, then cut diagonally in half *once*
One 2-1/2" x 42" strip; recut into four 2-1/2" squares
One 2-1/2" x 42" strip (for A and B pieces)

From the stripe, cut:
Two 6-1/2" x 34-1/2" *lengthwise* strips (for middle
  side border)
Three 6-1/2" x 29" *widthwise* strips (for middle top
  and bottom border)

From the lavender tonal, cut:
One 4-3/4" x 42" strip; recut into two 3-7/8" squares,
  then cut diagonally in half *once*; and three 4-3/4"
  squares
Two 2-1/2" x 42" strips; recut into three 2-1/2" x 21"
  strips (for strip sets)
Five 2-1/2" x 42" strips (for outer border)
Six 2-1/4" x 42" strips (for binding)

INSTRUCTIONS

Note: Use a 1/4" seam allowance throughout. Press
seams toward the darker fabric after adding each
piece or as indicated.

Nine-Patch Block Assembly

1. Following **Diagram 1** and using 2-1/2" x 21" strips, sew a lavender tonal strip lengthwise between two mottled green strips. Press seams toward the lavender strip. Crosscut six 2-1/2" wide segments (A). In the same manner, stitch a mottled green strip between two lavender tonal strips, then crosscut six 2-1/2" wide segments (B).

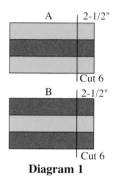

Diagram 1

2. Referring to the **Nine-Patch Block Diagrams**, sew the segments together to make two 6-1/2" x 6-1/2" green blocks and two 6-1/2" x 6-1/2" lavender blocks. Stitch five 2-1/2" blue print squares together with four 2-1/2" mottled dark cream squares to make the 6-1/2" x 6-1/2" blue block.

Green
Make 2

Lavender
Make 2

Blue
Make 1

Nine-Patch Block Diagrams

Big Dipper Block Assembly

1. Sew a 4-1/4" blue print triangle to a 4-1/4" mottled dark cream triangle as shown in **Diagram 2**. Make a total of 32 units.

Make 32

Diagram 2

2. Referring to the **Big Dipper Block Diagrams** and noting orientation, stitch two units together. Make a total of four sections, then sew the sections together to make one 6-1/2" x 6-1/2" block. Make a total of four blocks.

Make 4

Big Dipper Block Diagrams

Diamond Block Assembly

1. Trace the patterns provided for pieces A and B onto the template plastic. Cut out neatly and label. From the 2-1/2" x 42" blue print strip, cut eight A pieces, four B pieces, and four Br (reverse) pieces. From the 2-1/2" x 42" mottled dark cream strip, cut four A pieces, eight B pieces, and eight Br (reverse) pieces.

2. Following **Diagram 3**, sew a mottled dark cream B piece to one angled side of a blue print A piece and a mottled dark cream Br piece to the other angled side. Make a total of eight blue units. In the same manner, use blue print B and Br pieces and mottled dark cream A pieces to make four cream units.

B BR   B BR

Make 8   Make 4

Diagram 3

3. Stitch a 2-7/8" blue print triangle to a 2-7/8" mottled dark cream triangle. Make a total of 24 half-square triangle units.

4. Referring to the **Diamond Block Diagram**, sew six half-square triangle units together with two blue units and one cream unit into horizontal rows. Stitch the rows together to complete one 6-1/2" x 6-1/2" block. Make a total of four blocks.

Make 4
Diamond Block Diagram

Square-in-a-Square Block Assembly

1. Referring to the **Square-in-a-Square Block Diagrams**, sew a 3-7/8" mottled green triangle to each side of a 4-3/4" lavender tonal square to make one 6-1/2" x 6-1/2" lavender block. Make a total of three blocks.

Lavender
Make 3

Green
Make 1

Square-in-a-Square Block Diagrams

2. In the same manner, make one green block using four 3-7/8" lavender tonal triangles and a 4-3/4" mottled green square.

Appliqué Block Assembly

1. Using the patterns provided, trace the indicated number of shapes onto the fabrics designated on the patterns. Cut out neatly, adding a 1/8" to 1/4" seam allowance around each shape.

2. Turn the seam allowance under on each shape. Appliqué the shapes onto the 6-1/2" mottled dark cream squares, referring to the photo for placement. Trim away the background fabric behind the appliqué shapes if desired.

Quilt Assembly and Finishing

1. Referring to the **Quilt Layout Diagram** and noting block placement and orientation, sew the blocks together into five horizontal rows of five blocks each. (**Note:** The remaining blocks will be used in the middle border.) Stitch the rows together to complete the 30-1/2" x 30-1/2" quilt center.

2. *Inner border.* Sew the 2-1/2" x 30-1/2" tan tonal strips to the top and bottom of the quilt center and the 2-1/2" x 34-1/2" tan tonal strips to the sides. Press seams toward the strips.

3. *Middle border.* Stitch the 6-1/2" x 34-1/2" stripe strips to the sides of the quilt top. Sew the three 6-1/2" x 29" stripe strips short ends together to make one long strip. Cut two 34-1/2" lengths. Stitch a Big Dipper block to one end of one strip and a green Nine-Patch block to the other. Press seams toward the strip. Sew to the top of the quilt top. Stitch the remaining blocks to the ends of the other strip, then sew to the bottom of the quilt top. Press seams toward the strips.

4. *Outer border.* Stitch the five 2-1/2" x 42" lavender tonal strips short ends together to make one long strip. Cut two 46-1/2" lengths and two 50-1/2" lengths. Sew the shorter strips to the top and bottom of the quilt top and the longer strips to the sides. Press seams toward the strips.

5. Layer the quilt top right side up on top of the batting and the wrong side of the backing. Quilt as desired. Trim backing and batting even with the quilt top.

6. Bind as desired using the six 2-1/4" x 42" lavender tonal strips.

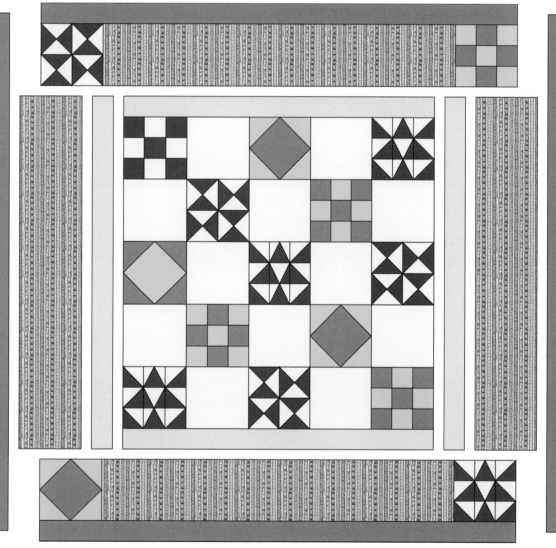

Quilt Layout Diagram

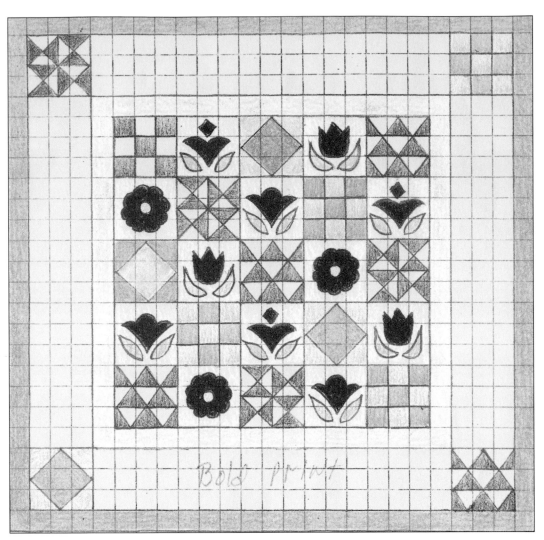

Jim Shore's hand drawing of quilt. ©JSHORE

Designed by Jan Shore • **Pieced by Angie Faulkenberry** • **Finished quilt size:** 50" x 50"

Friendship Pillows

I've always had a soft spot for teddy bears. And why not? Teddy bears are great. As a species, they don't eat much, are generally polite, and almost always have a pleasant disposition. There's an innocence in bears, a gentle quality that's always comforting and loves unconditionally. And, above all, there's a tradition of emotional attachment that inspires warm memories stretching back generations. In that way, they're a lot like quilts.

Jim Shore

When I started designing these pillows, I could have gone on forever. I love these designs and the way they work with several of the quilts in this book. This would be a great project to put together as a sampler quilt. Or keep it simple and let your children or grandchildren help with them.

Jan Shore

Skill level: Beginner
Finished pillow sizes: 12" x 12", 16" x 16"

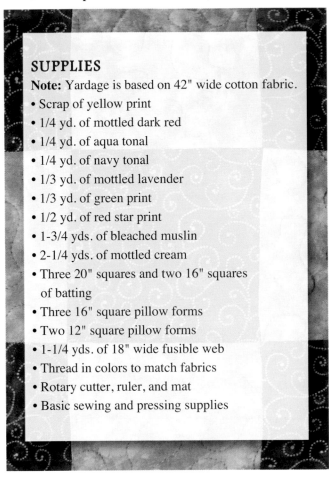

SUPPLIES

Note: Yardage is based on 42" wide cotton fabric.
- Scrap of yellow print
- 1/4 yd. of mottled dark red
- 1/4 yd. of aqua tonal
- 1/4 yd. of navy tonal
- 1/3 yd. of mottled lavender
- 1/3 yd. of green print
- 1/2 yd. of red star print
- 1-3/4 yds. of bleached muslin
- 2-1/4 yds. of mottled cream
- Three 20" squares and two 16" squares of batting
- Three 16" square pillow forms
- Two 12" square pillow forms
- 1-1/4 yds. of 18" wide fusible web
- Thread in colors to match fabrics
- Rotary cutter, ruler, and mat
- Basic sewing and pressing supplies

CUTTING INSTRUCTIONS

From the aqua tonal, cut:
One 4-7/8" x 42" strip; recut into five 4-7/8" squares, then cut diagonally in half

From the navy tonal, cut:
One 4-7/8" x 42" strip; recut into one 4-7/8" square, then cut diagonally in half; and five 4-1/2" squares

From the mottled lavender, cut:
One 4-7/8" x 42" strip; recut into two 4-7/8" squares, then cut diagonally in half; and five 4-1/2" squares

From the bleached muslin, cut:
Two 20" x 42" strips; recut into three 20" squares (for lining)
One 16" x 42" strip; recut into two 16" squares (for lining)

From the mottled cream, cut:
Three 16-1/2" x 42" strips; recut into two 16-1/2" squares and six 11" x 16-1/2" pieces
Two 12-1/2" x 42" strips; recut into one 12-1/2" square and four 9" x 12-1/2" pieces
One 4-7/8" x 42" strip; recut into five 4-7/8" squares, then cut diagonally in half; and three 4-1/2" squares

INSTRUCTIONS

Note: Use a 1/4" seam allowance throughout. Press seams toward the darker fabric after adding each piece or as indicated.

Nine-Patch Pillow

1. Following **Diagram 1**, sew the five 4-1/2" navy tonal squares together with four 4-1/2" mottled lavender squares into three horizontal rows. Stitch the rows together to complete the 12-1/2" x 12-1/2" pillow top.

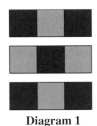

Diagram 1

2. Layer the pillow top right side up on top of one 16" batting square and the wrong side of one 16" muslin square. Baste and quilt as desired. Trim batting and backing even with the pillow top.

3. Turn one long edge of a 9" x 12-1/2" mottled cream piece under 1/4". Press. Turn under 1/4" again and stitch to hem. Repeat with a second 9" x 12-1/2"

mottled cream piece. Turn the quilted pillow top right side up. Place one hemmed strip right sides together with the pillow top, with outer edges aligned and the hemmed edge toward the center of the pillow top as shown in **Diagram 2**. Repeat with the second hemmed strip, overlapping the hemmed edges of the two strips. Pin the layers together. Sew around the outside edges. Trim the corners and turn right side out.

4. Insert a 12" square pillow form.

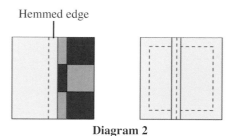

Diagram 2

Star Pillow

1. Use the 4-7/8" aqua tonal, mottled cream, mottled lavender, and navy tonal triangles to make the number of units indicated in **Diagram 3**.

Make 2   Make 7   Make 3

Diagram 3

2. Referring to **Diagram 4** and noting orientation, sew the units made in step 1 together with the three 4-1/2" mottled cream squares and the remaining 4-1/2" mottled lavender square into four horizontal rows. Stitch the rows together to complete the 16-1/2" x 16-1/2" pillow top.

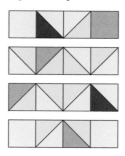

Diagram 4

3. Repeat steps 2 through 4 for the Nine-Patch Pillow, this time using 20" muslin lining and batting squares, two 11" x 16-1/2" mottled cream backing pieces, and a 16" square pillow form.

Tulip Pillow

1. Using the patterns provided, trace the tulip shapes onto the wrong side of the fusible web, leaving 1/2" between shapes. (**Note:** For reverse pieces, place the patterns face down and then trace.) Cut out roughly. Following manufacturer's directions,

fuse the shapes onto the wrong side of the fabrics designated on the patterns. Cut out neatly.

2. Referring to the photo for placement, remove the paper backing and arrange the shapes on a 16-1/2" mottled cream square. Fuse in place. Stitch all shapes in place using matching thread.

3. Repeat steps 2 through 4 for the Nine-Patch Pillow, this time using 20" muslin lining and batting squares, two 11" x 16-1/2" mottled cream backing pieces, and a 16" square pillow form.

Flower Pillow

1. Using the patterns provided, trace the flower shapes onto the wrong side of the fusible web, leaving 1/2" between shapes. (**Note:** For reverse pieces, place the patterns face down and then trace.) Cut out roughly. Fuse the shapes onto the wrong side of the fabrics designated on the patterns. Cut out neatly.

2. Referring to the photo for placement, remove the paper backing and arrange the shapes on a 16-1/2" mottled cream square. Fuse in place. Stitch all shapes in place using matching thread.

3. Repeat steps 2 through 4 for the Nine-Patch Pillow, this time using 20" muslin lining and batting squares, two 11" x 16-1/2" mottled cream backing pieces, and a 16" square pillow form.

Heart Pillow

1. Using the patterns provided, trace the heart shapes onto the wrong side of the fusible web, leaving 1/2" between shapes. (**Note:** For reverse pieces, place the patterns face down and then trace.) Cut out roughly. Fuse the shapes onto the wrong side of the fabrics designated on the patterns. Cut out neatly.

2. Referring to the photo for placement, remove the paper backing and arrange the shapes on a 12-1/2" mottled cream square. Fuse in place. Stitch all shapes in place using matching thread.

3. Repeat steps 2 through 4 for the Nine-Patch Pillow, this time using 16" muslin lining and batting squares, two 9" x 12-1/2" mottled cream backing pieces, and a 12" square pillow form.

Finished pillow size: 16" x 16"

Finished pillow size: 16" x 16"

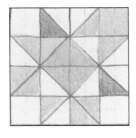

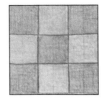

Jim Shore's hand drawings of pillows. ©JSHORE

Finished pillow size: 12" x 12"

Finished pillow size: 12" x 12"

Finished pillow size: 16" x 16"

**All pillows designed by Jan Shore
and pieced by Pine Tree Country Quilts**

A Mother's Love

Some of the most inspirational feedback I get is from mothers who find in my work some expression of the love they feel for their family. Their thoughts go to the heart of what I'm trying to do as an artist. I use patterns and images taken from the art that people have produced in their homes for centuries. A quilt isn't just a quilt. It's a piece of art Mom or Grandma worked to create that's become part of the history of the family, an heirloom. It means something special when mothers and daughters see the same designs in my art. It's a connection we share that continues back for generations.

Jim Shore

This quilt is really special to me. It reminds me of the love my mother and I shared. And now, the love I share with my daughters and son. Our family is truly blessed. We all live very close to each other. We are together constantly. Just imagine five daughters and one son and all the son-in-laws and grandchildren! There are 22 of us in all — I love it!.

Jan Shore.

Skill level: Intermediate
Block size sewn into quilt: 5-5/8" x 5-5/8"
Number of blocks: 72
Finished quilt size: 53" x 61"

SUPPLIES

Note: Yardage is based on 42" wide cotton fabric.
- 1/4 yd. of light green print
- 1/3 yd. of mottled dark lavender
- 3/8 yd. of medium pink print
- 5/8 yd. of light lavender print
- 1-1/2 yds. of light pink print
- 1-5/8 yds. of mottled dark red
- 2 yds. of mottled cream
- 61" x 69" piece of backing fabric
- 61" x 69" piece of *Fairfield* Nature-Fil Bamboo batting
- 4 yds. of 18" wide fusible web
- 1-1/2 yds. of white medium-weight fusible interfacing
- Thread in colors to match fabrics
- Rotary cutter, ruler, and mat
- Spray starch
- Basic sewing and pressing supplies

CUTTING INSTRUCTIONS

From the light pink print, cut:
Two 9-1/4" x 42" strips; recut into six 9-1/4" squares
    and two 4-7/8" squares
Five 6-1/8" x 42" strips; recut into thirty 6-1/8"
    squares

From the mottled dark red, cut:
Six 2-1/2" x 42" strips (for border)
Two 2-1/4" x 42" strips; recut into twenty-eight
    2-1/4" squares
Six 2-1/4" x 42" strips (for binding)
Twelve 1-1/2" x 42" strips; recut into three hundred
    ten 1-1/2" squares

From the mottled cream, cut:
One 26" x 42" piece; recut into one 26" square
    (for appliqué) and eight 6-1/8" squares
Six 6-1/8" x 42" strips; recut into thirty-four
    6-1/8" squares

INSTRUCTIONS

Note: Use a 1/4" seam allowance throughout. Press seams toward the darker fabric after adding each piece or as indicated.

Snowball Block Assembly

1. Draw a diagonal line on the wrong side of each 1-1/2" mottled dark red square. Referring to the **Block Diagrams**, place a marked square on each corner of a 6-1/8" mottled cream square. Sew on the drawn lines, trim seam allowance to 1/4", then press seams toward the triangles to complete one block.

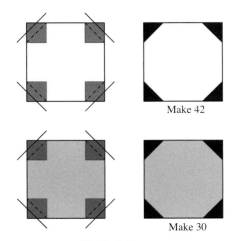

Make 42

Make 30

Block Diagrams

2. Repeat step 1 to make a total of 42 cream blocks. In the same manner, make a total of 30 pink blocks, this time using marked 1-1/2" dark red squares and 6-1/8" light pink print squares. (**Note:** Set aside the remaining marked squares for use in the side units and corner units.)

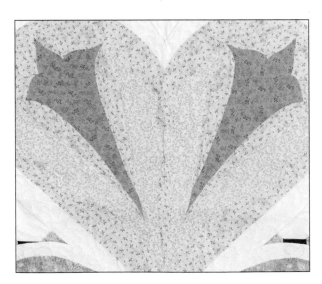

Side and Corner Unit Assembly

1. Draw a diagonal line on the wrong side of each 2-1/4" mottled dark red square. Following **Diagram 1**, place a marked square on each corner of a 9-1/4" light pink square. Sew on the drawn lines, trim seam allowance to 1/4", then press seams toward the triangles. Make a total of six units.

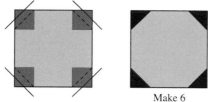

Make 6

Diagram 1

2. Apply a liberal coat of spray starch to each unit and press dry. Cut each unit diagonally in half twice to yield 24 triangles. (**Note:** Handle the triangles carefully until stitched into the quilt to avoid stretching the bias edges.)

3. Place a marked 1-1/2" mottled red square set aside in step 2 of the Snowball Block Assembly to the remaining corner of each unit as shown in **Diagram 2**. Stitch on the drawn lines, trim seam allowance to 1/4", then press seams toward the triangles to complete the side units.

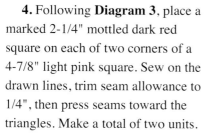

Diagram 2

4. Following **Diagram 3**, place a marked 2-1/4" mottled dark red square on each of two corners of a 4-7/8" light pink square. Sew on the drawn lines, trim seam allowance to 1/4", then press seams toward the triangles. Make a total of two units.

Make 2

Diagram 3

5. Apply a liberal coat of spray starch to each unit and press dry. Cut each unit diagonally in half once through the triangles to yield four corner units, again handling the triangles carefully.

Quilt Assembly and Finishing

1. Referring to the **Quilt Center Diagram**, sew the cream blocks, pink blocks, side units, and corner units together into 12 diagonal rows. Press seams toward the pink blocks. Stitch the rows together, matching all seams, and square up the quilt center to measure 48-1/2" x 56-1/2".

2. *Border*. Sew the six 2-1/2" x 42" mottled dark red strips short ends together to make one long strip. Cut two 56-1/2" lengths and two 52-1/2" lengths. Following the **Quilt Layout Diagram**, stitch the longer strips to the long sides of the quilt center and the shorter strips to the other sides. Press seams away from the quilt center.

Quilt Center Diagram

3. *Appliqués.* Following manufacturer's directions, apply fusible interfacing to the wrong side of the 26" mottled cream square. Using the patterns provided, trace the indicated number of appliqué shapes onto the paper side of the fusible web, leaving at least 1/2" between shapes. (**Note:** For reverse pieces, place the templates face down and then trace.) Cut out roughly. Following manufacturer's directions, fuse the shapes onto the wrong side of the fabrics designated on the patterns. Cut out neatly. Referring to the photo for placement, arrange the small hearts on the block centers. Fuse in place. Position the large heart motif on the bottom left corner of the quilt center. Fuse in place. Stitch all shapes in place using matching thread.

4. Layer the quilt top right side up on top of the batting and the wrong side of the backing. Quilt as desired. Trim backing and batting even with the quilt top.

5. Bind as desired using the six 2-1/4" x 42" mottled dark red strips.

Quilt Layout Diagram

Jim Shore's hand drawing of quilt. ©JSHORE

Designed by Kathy Atwell • Pieced by Pine Tree Country Quilts • Finished quilt size: 53" x 61"

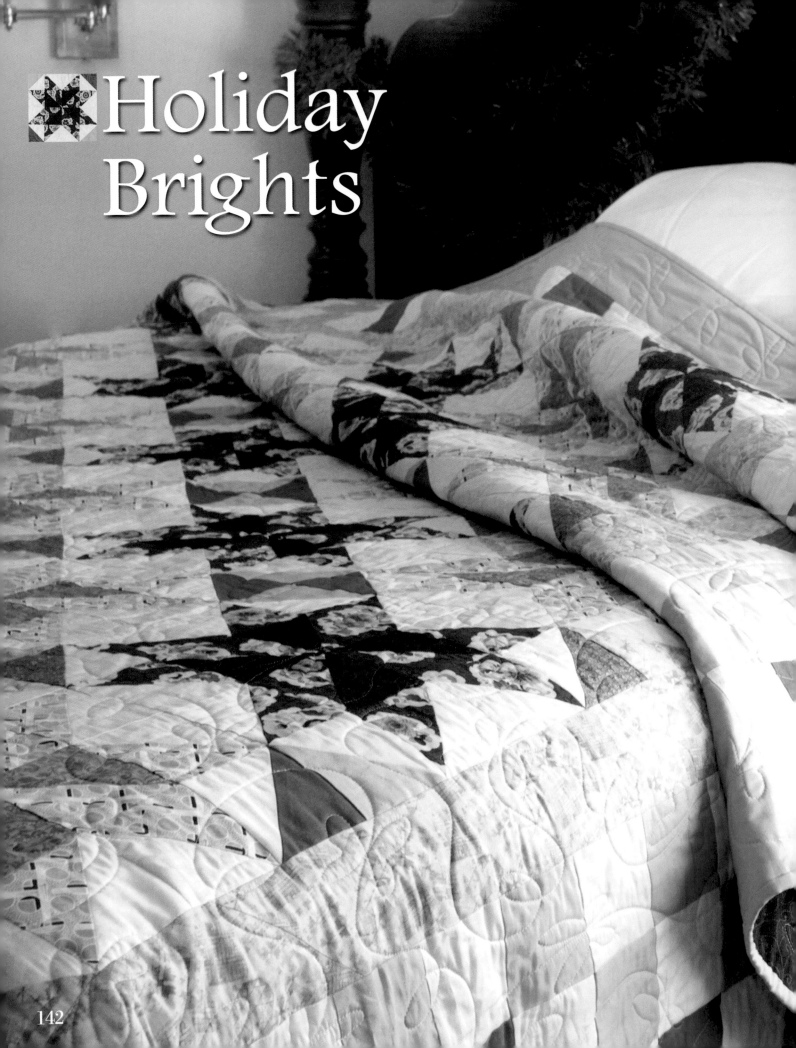

Holiday Brights

If I have said this before, please forgive me, but the color in this quilt is outta this world! I love all the brights put together. It's unexpected, yet it somehow works. So just mix and match to your heart's content.

Jan Shore

North Star

The North Star arrives bright and shining, toys all packed for their delivery

I love my work. And though Santa Claus is one of my favorite images, the subject doesn't really matter. The process is pretty much the same. First I take great care in crafting the shape of each piece, adhering to folk art forms and styling that go back generations. Then comes the fun part: decorating with the complex combination of colors and patterns that have their roots in quilting, appliqué and rosemaling. My challenge is to blend these traditions to create authentic works of art that are completely new yet grounded in our past. That keeps me energized.

Jim Shore

143

Skill level: Beginner
Block size sewn into quilt: 12" x 12"
Number of blocks: 30
Finished quilt size: 90" x 102"

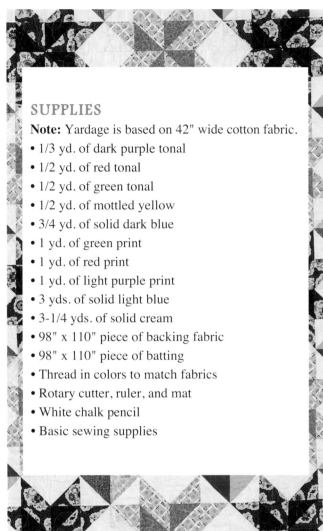

SUPPLIES

Note: Yardage is based on 42" wide cotton fabric.

- 1/3 yd. of dark purple tonal
- 1/2 yd. of red tonal
- 1/2 yd. of green tonal
- 1/2 yd. of mottled yellow
- 3/4 yd. of solid dark blue
- 1 yd. of green print
- 1 yd. of red print
- 1 yd. of light purple print
- 3 yds. of solid light blue
- 3-1/4 yds. of solid cream
- 98" x 110" piece of backing fabric
- 98" x 110" piece of batting
- Thread in colors to match fabrics
- Rotary cutter, ruler, and mat
- White chalk pencil
- Basic sewing supplies

CUTTING INSTRUCTIONS

From the dark purple tonal, cut:
Two 3-7/8" x 42" strips; recut into fifteen
    3-7/8" squares

From the red tonal, cut:
Three 3-7/8" x 42" strips; recut into thirty
    3-7/8" squares

From the green tonal, cut:
Three 3-7/8" x 42" strips; recut into thirty
    3-7/8" squares

From the mottled yellow, cut:
Three 3-7/8" x 42" strips; recut into twenty-five
    3-7/8" squares

From the solid dark blue, cut:
Two 3-7/8" x 42" strips; recut into fifteen
    3-7/8" squares
Four 3-1/2" x 42" strips; recut into forty-four
    3-1/2" squares

From the green print, cut:
Nine 3-7/8" x 42" strips; recut into ninety
    3-7/8" squares

From the red print, cut:
Nine 3-7/8" x 42" strips; recut into ninety
   3-7/8" squares

From the light purple print, cut:
Two 3-7/8" x 42" strips; recut into fifteen
   3-7/8" squares
Seven 3-1/2" x 42" strips (for inner border)

From the solid light blue, cut:
Two 3-7/8" x 42" strips; recut into fifteen
   3-7/8" squares
Ten 3-1/2" x 42" strips; recut into one hundred
   eighteen 3-1/2" squares
Nine 3-1/2" x 42" strips (for outer border)
Ten 2-1/4" x 42" strips (for binding)

From the solid cream, cut:
Sixteen 3-7/8" x 42" strips; recut into one hundred
   fifty-five 3-7/8" squares
Fourteen 3-1/2" x 42" strips; recut into one hundred
   sixty-two 3-1/2" squares

INSTRUCTIONS

Note: Use a 1/4" seam allowance throughout. Press
seams toward the darker fabric after adding each piece
or as indicated.

Quilt Center Assembly

1. Use the chalk pencil to draw a diagonal line on
the wrong side of the 3-7/8" green print, red print,
light purple print, dark purple tonal, and light blue

print squares. Following **Diagram 1**, place a marked
green print square right sides together with a marked
green tonal square. Sew 1/4" away from each side
of the drawn line, cut apart on the line, and press
open. Repeat to make a total of 60 units. In the same
manner, make the following number of half-square
triangle units: 60 red print/red tonal, 100 green
print/solid cream, 20 green print/mottled yellow,
94 red print/mottled cream, 26 red print/mottled
yellow, 27 light purple/mottled cream, 3 light pur-
ple/mottled yellow, 29 dark purple/mottled cream,
1 dark purple/mottled yellow, 30 light blue/mottled
cream, 29 dark blue/mottled cream, and 1 dark
blue/mottled yellow.

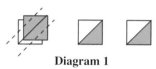

Diagram 1

2. Referring to the **Block Diagrams** for assembly
and the **Quilt Layout Diagram** for suggested color
placement, stitch 16 units together to make one
12-1/2" x 12-1/2" block. Make a total of 15 green
blocks and 15 red blocks.

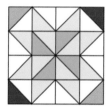

Make 15   Make 15
Block Diagrams

Quilt Layout Diagram

Quilt Assembly and Finishing

1. Referring to the **Quilt Layout Diagram**, sew the blocks together into six horizontal rows of five blocks each. Stitch the rows together to complete the 60-1/2" x 72-1/2" quilt center.

2. *Inner border.* Sew the seven 3-1/2" x 42" light purple print strips short ends together to make one long strip. Cut two 72-1/2" lengths and two 66-1/2" lengths. Stitch the longer strips to the long sides of the quilt center and the shorter strips to the other sides. Press seams toward the border.

3. *Middle (pieced) border.* Alternating 3-1/2" solid cream squares with a random assortment of 3-1/2" solid light blue and solid dark blue squares, sew 26 rows of three squares each. Stitch the rows together matching all seams. Repeat to make a second strip unit, then sew to the long sides of the quilt top. In the same manner, stitch 28 rows of three squares each, then sew together. Repeat to make a second strip unit, then stitch to the other sides of the quilt top.

4. *Outer border.* Sew the nine 3-1/2" x 42" solid light blue strips short ends together to make one long strip. Cut two 96-1/2" lengths and two 90-1/2" lengths. Stitch the longer strips to the long sides of the quilt top and the shorter strips to the other sides.

5. Layer the quilt top right side up on top of the batting and the wrong side of the backing. Quilt as desired. Trim backing and batting even with the quilt top.

6. Bind as desired using the ten 2-1/4" x 42" solid light blue strips.

Jim Shore's hand drawing of quilt. ©JSHORE

Designed by Jan Shore • Pieced by Iva Mintz • Finished quilt size: 90" x 102"

Spring Is Here

A lot of my work is based on the culture and art of the Pennsylvania Dutch. These disciplined, hard-working people were thrust into a harsh and unforgiving wilderness on the edge of the known world. And yet they gave America some of its most enduring artistic traditions and beloved cultural icons, including St. Nick and the Easter Bunny. Not to mention some of the most popular quilt designs, including the Flower Basket.

Jim Shore

Could these bunnies and eggs get any cuter? Sometimes I look at Jim's figurines and I just wonder how he does it. Being able to make quilts using his drawings and figurines as inspiration is truly an honor. This quilt turned out just great. I love the graphics, using hard lines to make soft flowers.

Jan Shore

Skill level: Advanced
Block size sewn into quilt: 10" x 12", 6" x 6"
Number of blocks: 10
Finished quilt size: 46" x 56"

SUPPLIES

Note: Yardage is based on 42" wide cotton fabric.
- 1/8 yd. of pink print
- 1/8 yd. of dark pink tonal
- 1/4 yd. of light green tonal
- 1/4 yd. of yellow/white print
- 1/4 yd. of mottled cream
- 1/3 yd. of medium blue tonal
- 1/3 yd. of dark sage green tonal
- 1/2 yd. of peach print
- 1/2 yd. of lavender print
- 1/2 yd. of dark yellow tonal
- 1/2 yd. of light aqua/white print
- 3/4 yd. of light blue tonal
- 1-1/2 yds. of medium sage green tonal
- 54" x 64" piece of backing fabric
- 54" x 64" piece of batting
- Thread in colors to match fabrics
- Rotary cutter, ruler, and mat
- Foundation paper or photocopy paper
- Basic sewing supplies

CUTTING INSTRUCTIONS

From the pink print, cut:
One 2-7/8" x 42" strip; recut into nine 2-7/8" squares, then cut diagonally in half *once*; and three 2-1/2" x 4-1/2" pieces

From the dark pink tonal, cut:
One 2-7/8" x 42" strip; recut into twelve 2-7/8" squares, then cut diagonally in half *once*; and three 2-1/2" squares

From the light green tonal, cut:
One 4-1/2" x 42" strip; recut into four 4-1/2" squares and four 2-1/2" squares

From the yellow/white print, cut:
One 4-1/2" x 42" strip; recut into fifteen 2-1/2" x 4-1/2" pieces and one 2-1/2" square

From the mottled cream, cut:
One 3-1/4" x 42" strip; recut into five 3-1/4" squares, then cut diagonally in half *twice*
One 2-7/8" x 42" strip; recut into eight 2-7/8" squares, then cut diagonally in half *once*; and three 2-1/2" squares

From the medium blue tonal, cut:
One 4-7/8" x 42" strip; recut into one 4-7/8" square, then cut diagonally in half *once*; four 3-1/4" squares, then cut diagonally in half *twice*; three 2-7/8" squares, then cut diagonally in half *once*; and two 2-1/4" x 3-3/4" pieces
One 2-1/2" x 42" strip; recut into two 2-1/2" x 12-1/2" strips, two 2-1/2" x 4-1/2" pieces, and two 2-1/2" squares

From the dark sage green tonal, cut:
Three 2-1/2" x 42" strips (for strip sets)

From the peach print, cut:
Three 2-1/2" x 42" strips (for strip sets)
One 2-1/2" x 42" strip; recut into three 2-1/2" squares and six 2-1/2" x 6-1/2" pieces
One 2-1/4" x 42" strip; recut into six 2-1/4" x 3-3/4" pieces

From the lavender print, cut:
Three 2-1/2" x 42" strips (for strip sets)
Three 2-1/2" x 42" strips; recut into three 2-1/2" x
    4-1/2" pieces and twenty-eight 2-1/2" squares

From the dark yellow tonal, cut:
One 4-1/2" x 42" strip; recut into fifteen 2-1/2" x
    4-1/2" pieces
One 3-1/4" x 42" strip; recut into two 3-1/4" squares,
    then cut diagonally in half *twice*; and five
    2-1/2" squares
One 2-7/8" x 42" strip; recut into eleven 2-7/8"
    squares, then cut diagonally in half *once*

From the light aqua/white print, cut:
Two 2-1/2" x 42" strips; recut into twenty-eight
    2-1/2" squares
Three 2-1/4" x 42" strips; recut into twenty-eight
    2-1/4" x 3-3/4" pieces

From the light blue tonal, cut:
One 4-7/8" x 42" strip; recut into two 4-7/8" squares,
    then cut diagonally in half *once*; and four 4-1/2" x
    6-1/2" pieces
One 3-1/2" x 42" strip; recut into eight 3-1/2" squares
One 2-7/8" x 42" strip; recut into six 2-7/8" squares,
    then cut diagonally in half *once*
Three 2-1/2" x 42" strips; recut into four 2-1/2" x
    12-1/2" strips, six 2-1/2" x 4-1/2" pieces, and
    sixteen 2-1/2" squares
One 2-1/4" x 42" strip; recut into ten 2-1/4" x
    3-3/4" pieces

From the medium sage green tonal, cut:
Three 2-1/2" x 42" strips (for strip sets)
Ten 2-1/2" x 42" strips (for sashing and border)
Six 2-1/4" x 42" strips (for binding)

INSTRUCTIONS

Note: Use a 1/4" seam allowance throughout. Press
seams toward the darker fabric after adding each piece
or as indicated.

Cutting the Paper-Piecing Triangles
1. Following **Diagram 1**, cut fourteen 2-1/4" x
3-3/4" light aqua/white print pieces in half to make triangles for paper piecing. Cut the remaining light
aqua/white print pieces in half as shown to make
reverse triangles.

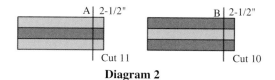

Cut 14 light aqua
Cut 5 light blue
Cut 1 medium blue
Cut 3 peach

Cut 14 light aqua
Cut 5 light blue
Cut 1 medium blue
Cut 3 peach

Reverse

Diagram 1

2. Repeat step 1 with the 2-1/4" x 3-3/4" light
blue tonal pieces to cut five triangles and five reverse
triangles, with the 2-1/4" x 3-3/4" medium blue tonal
pieces to cut one triangle and one reverse triangle,
and with the 2-1/4" x 3-3/4" peach print pieces to cut
three triangles and three reverse triangles.

Section 1 Assembly
1. Following **Diagram 2** and using 2-1/2" x 42"
strips, sew a lavender print strip lengthwise between
two peach print strips. Crosscut eleven 2-1/2" wide
segments (A). In the same manner, stitch a peach
print strip lengthwise between two lavender print
strips and crosscut ten 2-1/2" wide segments (B).

A | 2-1/2"   B | 2-1/2"

Cut 11   Cut 10

Diagram 2

2. Referring to the **Quilt Layout Diagram**, sew
the A segments alternately together with the B segments to complete the 6-1/2" x 42-1/2" Section 1.

Section 2 Assembly
1. Draw a diagonal line on the wrong side of
each 4-1/2" light green tonal square. Following
Diagram 3, place a marked square right sides
together on one end of a 4-1/2" x 6-1/2" light blue
tonal piece. Sew on the drawn line, trim seam
allowance to 1/4", and press the triangle open to
make one leaf unit. Repeat to make a second unit.
Also make two reverse leaf units.

Reverse

Make 2   Make 2

Diagram 3

2. Draw a diagonal line on the wrong side of each of twelve 2-1/2" light blue tonal squares. Place a marked square right sides together on each end of a 2-1/2" x 6-1/2" peach print piece as shown in **Diagram 4**. Stitch on the drawn lines, trim seam allowance to 1/4", and press the triangles open to make one tulip side unit. Make a total of three units. Also make three reverse tulip side units.

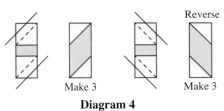

Diagram 4

3. Make three copies of the tulip center paper-piecing pattern and four copies of the sashing paper-piecing pattern. Place a 2-1/2" x 4-1/2" lavender print piece right side up on the unmarked side of the tulip center paper-piecing pattern and pin in place. Lay the pinned unit on a light box or bright window and mark a line on the fabric 1/4" beyond the seam line between the center diamond and the corner triangles. Trim the fabric beyond the drawn lines as shown in **Diagram 5**.

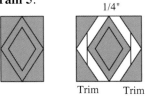

Diagram 5

4. Place a light blue paper-piecing triangle right sides together on the upper left edge of the lavender diamond (see **Diagram 6**). Pin in place. Flip the pattern over and sew on the line between the diamond and corner triangle sections, extending the stitching to the outer edges of the pattern. Fold the triangle over to be sure it completely covers the triangle and outer seam allowance area. Press. Repeat with a light blue reverse triangle on the upper right edge of the diamond, then with a peach triangle and peach reverse triangle on the remaining edges of the diamond. Trim the fabric even with the outer edges of the pattern all the way around. Sew a 2-1/2" peach print square to the peach end to complete one tulip center unit. Make a total of three units.

   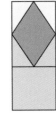

Diagram 6

Make 3

5. Using the sashing paper-piecing patterns with the 2-1/2" light green tonal squares for the center section and 3-1/2" light blue tonal squares for the end sections, make four outer sashing pieces. Following **Diagram 7** and noting orientation, stitch a 2-1/2" x 4-1/2" light blue tonal piece between two outer sashing pieces. Repeat to make a second sashing unit.

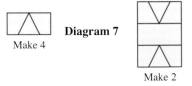

Make 4   Diagram 7

Make 2

6. Referring to the **Quilt Layout Diagram**, sew the units together to complete the 6-1/2" x 42-1/2" Section 2.

Section 3 Assembly

1. Following **Diagram 8**, sew five 2-1/2" x 4-1/2" yellow/white print pieces alternately together with five 2-1/2" x 4-1/2" dark yellow tonal pieces. Stitch a 2-1/2" dark yellow tonal square to the left end of the pieced strip. Repeat to make a second strip.

2. Sew five 2-1/2" x 4-1/2" dark yellow tonal pieces alternately together with five 2-1/2" x 4-1/2"

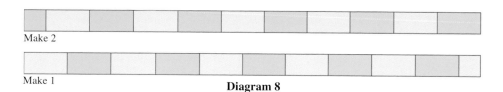

Make 2

Make 1

Diagram 8

yellow/white print pieces. Stitch the 2-1/2" yellow/white print square to the right end of the pieced strip.

3. Referring to the **Quilt Layout Diagram**, sew the pieced strips alternately together to complete the 6-1/2" x 42-1/2" Section 3.

Section 4 Assembly

1. Make three copies of the point paper-piecing pattern. Use the light blue paper-piecing triangles, light blue reverse triangles, medium blue triangles, medium blue reverse triangles, and 2-1/2" dark pink tonal squares to make one medium blue point unit and two light blue point units as shown in **Diagram 9**.

Make 2   Make 1

Diagram 9

2. Following **Diagram 10**, sew a 2-7/8" dark yellow tonal triangle to a 2-7/8" mottled cream triangle. Make a total of 15 yellow units. In the same manner, make a total of twelve dark pink/pink units, eight dark pink/light blue units, four dark pink/medium blue units, four pink/light blue units, and two pink/medium blue units.

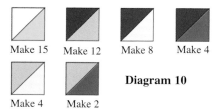

Make 15   Make 12   Make 8   Make 4

Make 4   Make 2

Diagram 10

3. Stitch a 3-1/4" dark yellow tonal triangle to a 3-1/4" mottled cream triangle (see **Diagram 11**). Make a total of six units.

Make 6

Diagram 11

4. Draw a diagonal line on the wrong side of each of the three 2-1/2" dark yellow tonal squares and three 2-1/2" mottled cream squares. Following **Diagram 12**, place a marked dark yellow square right sides together on one end of a 2-1/2" x 4-1/2" light blue tonal piece. Sew on the drawn line, trim seam allowance to 1/4", and press the triangle open. Repeat to make a second light blue/dark yellow unit and one medium blue/dark yellow unit. Also make two mottled cream/light blue reverse units and one mottled cream/medium blue reverse unit as shown.

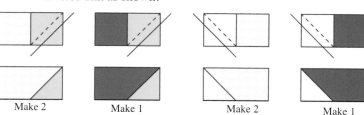

Make 2   Make 1   Make 2   Make 1

Diagram 12

5. Stitch the units together as shown in **Diagram 13** to make three block bottom rows. Press seams away from the triangle/square.

Make 2   **Diagram 13**   Make 1

6. Following **Diagram 14**, sew three yellow triangle/squares together with one half-square unit and one 2-7/8" dark yellow triangle. Press seams away from the center triangle/square. Stitch one yellow triangle/square and one 2-7/8" dark yellow triangle together with one half-square unit. Press seams toward the center triangle square. Sew the two pieced strips together to make one basket unit. Make a total of three units. Stitch a 4-7/8" light blue tonal triangle to each end of two of the basket units and a 4-7/8" medium blue tonal triangle to each end of the remaining basket unit to complete the block center rows.

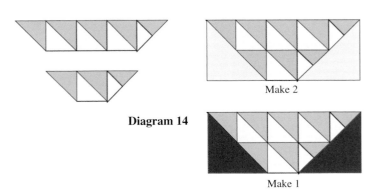

Diagram 14

Make 2

Make 1

7. Sew two dark pink/light blue triangle/squares together and two dark pink/pink triangle/squares together (see **Diagram 15**). Repeat to make one reverse unit. Stitch the two units together with a 2-1/2" x 4-1/2" pink piece. Press seams toward the pink piece. Sew a pink/light blue triangle/square to each of two opposite sides of a light blue point unit, then stitch a light blue square to each end. Press seams toward the squares. Sew the sections together to complete a light blue block top row, then repeat to make a second row. In the same manner, use dark pink, pink, and medium blue pieces to make one medium blue block top row.

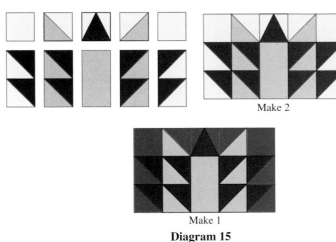

Make 2

Make 1

Diagram 15

8. Referring to the **Block Diagrams**, stitch the light blue block top, center, and bottom rows together to complete one light blue block. Repeat to make a second light blue block and one medium blue block.

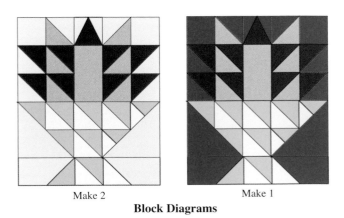

Make 2

Make 1

Block Diagrams

9. Following the **Quilt Layout Diagram**, sew the blocks alternately together with the 2-1/2" x 12-1/2" light blue tonal strips and 2-1/2" x 12-1/2" medium blue tonal strips to complete the 12-1/2" x 42-1/2" Section 4. Press seams toward the medium blue strips.

Section 5 Assembly

1. Make 28 copies of the point paper-piecing pattern. Using light aqua/white print paper-piecing triangles and reverse triangles and the 2-1/2" lavender print squares, make a total of 28 lavender point units as shown in **Diagram 16**.

Make 28
Diagram 16

2. Following **Diagram 17**, sew a 3-1/4" medium blue triangle to a 3-1/4" mottled cream triangle. Make a total of 14 units. Stitch two units together to make one center unit. Make a total of seven units.

Make 14
Make 7
Diagram 17

3. Referring to the **Star Block Diagrams**, sew the units together with four 2-1/2" light aqua/white print squares to complete one block. Press seams away from the center section. Make a total of seven blocks.

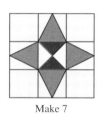
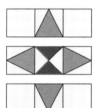
Make 7

Star Block Diagrams

4. Stitch the blocks together as shown in the **Quilt Layout Diagram** to complete the 6-1/2" x 42-1/2" Section 5.

Section 6 Assembly

1. Following **Diagram 18** and using 2-1/2" x 42" strips, sew a dark sage green tonal strip lengthwise between two medium sage green tonal strips. Cross-cut eleven 2-1/2" wide segments (C). In the same manner, stitch a medium sage green strip lengthwise between two dark sage strips and crosscut ten 2-1/2" segments (D).

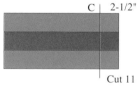
C | 2-1/2"
Cut 11

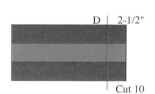
D | 2-1/2"
Cut 10

Diagram 18

2. Referring to the **Quilt Layout Diagram**, sew the segments alternately together to complete the 6-1/2" x 42-1/2" Section 6.

Quilt Assembly and Finishing

1. *Sashing and border.* Sew the ten 2-1/2" x 42" medium sage green tonal strips short ends together to make one long strip. Press seams in one direction. Cut seven 42-1/2" lengths and two 56-1/2" lengths. Referring to the **Quilt Layout Diagram**, stitch the shorter strips alternately together with the sections. Press seams toward the strips. Sew the longer strips to the sides of the quilt center. Press seams toward the strips.

2. Layer the quilt top right side up on top of the batting and the wrong side of the backing. Quilt as desired. Trim backing and batting even with the quilt top.

3. Bind as desired using the six 2-1/4" x 42" medium sage green tonal strips.

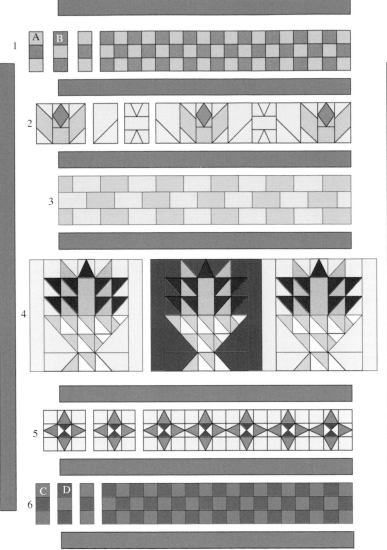

Quilt Layout Diagram

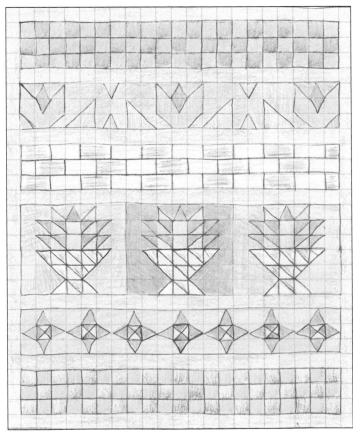

Jim Shore's hand drawing of quilt. ©JSHORE

Designed by Jan Shore • **Pieced by Pine Tree Country Quilts** • **Finished quilt size:** 46" x 56"

 Kitty Cabin

I wasn't always crazy about cats. I just couldn't get used to the idea of giving room and board to some animal that thought it was better than I was. But proximity over the years has turned loathing into first respect, then love. Now I find them great subject matter. All cats are perfect in their own way. Or at least they think they are.

Jim Shore

There is no way I could put together a quilt book and leave out the log cabin. Log cabin quilts, without a doubt, are the most beautiful of all quilts. Jim and I both agree on this, so it has to be true. I am amazed when I am looking at a couple of the old log cabins that I have. I love the different ways they are put together.

Jan Shore

Skill level: Intermediate
Block size sewn into quilt: 7" x 7"
Number of blocks: 42
Finished quilt size: 55" x 62"

SUPPLIES

Note: Yardage is based on 42" wide cotton fabric.

- 1/3 yd. of red tonal
- 1/3 yd. of medium cream tonal
- 5/8 yd. of dark brown tonal
- 5/8 yd. of golden brown print
- 5/8 yd. of solid rust
- 2/3 yd. of dark cream tonal
- 7/8 yd. of mottled lavender
- 1-1/8 yds. of green tonal
- 1-1/3 yds. of mottled light cream
- 63" x 70" piece of backing fabric
- 63" x 70" piece of batting
- 1-1/3 yds. of 18" wide fusible web
- 10 yds. of 1/4" wide fusible web tape
- 3/8" bias bar
- Thread in colors to match fabrics
- Rotary cutter, ruler, and mat
- Basic sewing and pressing supplies

CUTTING INSTRUCTIONS

From the red tonal, cut:
Two 1-1/2" x 42" strips; recut into forty-two
    1-1/2" squares (1)

From the medium cream tonal, cut:
Five 1-1/2" x 42" strips; recut into forty-two 1-1/2"
    squares (2) and forty-two 1-1/2" x 2-1/2"
    pieces (3)

From the dark brown tonal, cut:
Eleven 1-1/2" x 42" strips; recut into eighteen 1-1/2"
    x 2-1/2" pieces (4B), twenty-four 1-1/2" x 3-1/2"
    pieces (5A), eighteen 1-1/2" x 5-1/2" pieces (9B),
    and twenty-four 1-1/2" x 7-1/2" pieces (13A)

From the golden brown print, cut:
Eleven 1-1/2" x 42" strips; recut into eighteen 1-1/2"
    x 3-1/2" pieces (5B), twenty-four 1-1/2" x 4-1/2"
    pieces (8A), twenty-four 1-1/2" x 5-1/2" pieces
    (9A), and eighteen 1-1/2" x 6-1/2" pieces (12B)

From the solid rust, cut:
Twelve 1-1/2" x 42" strips; recut into twenty-four
    1-1/2" x 2-1/2" pieces (4A), eighteen 1-1/2" x
    4-1/2" pieces (8B), twenty-four 1-1/2" x 6-1/2"
    pieces (12A), and eighteen 1-1/2" x 7-1/2"
    pieces (13B)

From the dark cream tonal, cut:
Thirteen 1-1/2" x 42" strips; recut into forty-two
    1-1/2" x 5-1/2" pieces (10) and forty-two 1-1/2" x
    6-1/2" pieces (11)

From the mottled lavender, cut:
Six 1-1/2" x 42" strips (for outer border)
Six 2-1/2" x 42" strips (for binding)

From the green tonal, cut:
One 22" x 42" piece (for bias stems and vine)

From the mottled light cream, cut:
Nine 1-1/2" x 42" strips; recut into forty-two 1-1/2" x
    3-1/2" pieces (6) and forty-two 1-1/2" x 4-1/2"
    pieces (7)
Five 6" x 42" strips (for inner border)

INSTRUCTIONS

Note: Use a 1/4" seam allowance throughout. Press seams toward the darker fabric after adding each piece or as indicated.

Log Cabin Block Assembly

1. Following the **Block Diagrams**, sew a piece 2 to the bottom of a piece 1. Stitch a piece 3 to the left side, then sew a piece 4A to the top. Press seams toward the last piece added as you work. Continue adding pieces in a clockwise fashion to complete one 7-1/2" x 7-1/2" block.

2. Repeat step 1 to make a total of 24 A blocks, then make a total of 18 B blocks in the same manner using the pieces indicated.

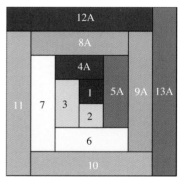

Block A   Make 24

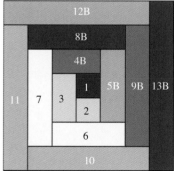

Block B   Make 18

Block Diagrams

Quilt Assembly

1. Referring to the **Quilt Layout Diagram**, sew six A blocks together. Press seams toward the dark brown pieces. Make a total of four rows. Stitch six B blocks together. Press seams toward the dark cream tonal pieces. Make a total of three rows. Sew the rows together to complete the 42-1/2" x 49-1/2" quilt center.

2. *Inner border.* Stitch the five 6" x 42" mottled light cream strips short ends together to make one long strip. Cut two 49-1/2" lengths and two 53-1/2" lengths. Sew the shorter strips to the short sides of the quilt center and the longer strips to the other sides. Press seams toward the strips.

3. *Outer border.* Stitch the six 1-1/2" x 42" mottled lavender strips short ends together to make one long strip. Cut two 60-1/2" lengths and two 55-1/2" lengths. Sew the longer strips to the long sides of the quilt top and the shorter strips to the other sides. Press seams toward the strips.

Appliqué

1. Using the patterns provided, trace the indicated number of shapes onto the paper side of the fusible web, leaving at least 1/2" between shapes. Cut out roughly. Following manufacturer's directions, fuse the shapes onto the wrong side of the fabrics designated on the patterns. Cut out neatly.

2. Following **Diagram 1**, trim one short end of the 22" x 42" green tonal piece at a 45° angle. Cut enough 1-1/2" bias strips to equal 360". Sew the strips short ends together to make one long strip. Fold the strip lengthwise in half with wrong sides together. Stitch along the raw edges using a *scant* 1/4" seam allowance. Trim seam allowance to 1/8". Flatten the strip with the seam centered on one side. Insert the bias bar into the strip and press the strip flat to make the vine piece. Apply fusible web tape along the center of the seam side of the vine piece. Remove the paper backing. Cut twenty-eight 3" pieces from the vine piece for stems.

3. Referring to the photo for placement, arrange the vines on the inner border strips. Trim excess at the end, leaving 1/4" to turn in on one end. Turn in 1/4" on one end and cover the raw edge of the remaining end. Fuse in place.

4. Remove the paper backing and arrange the shapes along the vine. Tuck the ends of the stems under the flower cups and the vine. Fuse in place.

5. Stitch all shapes in place using matching thread.

Quilt Finishing

1. Layer the quilt top right side up on top of the batting and the wrong side of the backing. Quilt as desired. Trim backing and batting even with the quilt top.

2. Bind as desired using the six 2-1/2" x 42" mottled lavender strips.

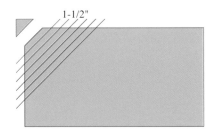

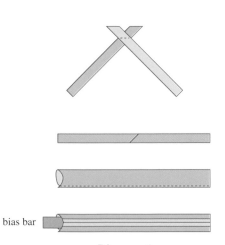

1-1/2"

bias bar

Diagram 1

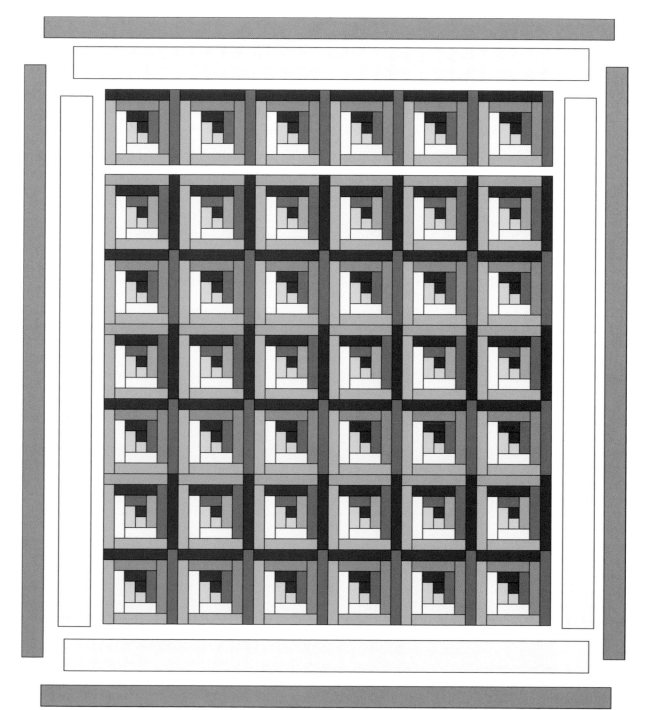

Quilt Layout Diagram

Jim Shore's hand drawing of quilt. ©JSHORE

Designed by Jim and Jan Shore • Pieced by Judy Neal • Finished quilt size: 55" x 62"

From This Day Forward

With five married daughters, I have a great deal of experience when it comes to playing Father of the Bride. Both my tuxedo and my wallet could use a rest. But each time I've walked down the aisle with one of my daughters, I've experienced a moment so precious, a pride so deep, I wouldn't trade being a father for anything in the world. My wedding angel is a portrait of my most beautiful daughter— each and every one of them.

Jim Shore

You are going to be reading the words "I love this quilt" repeatedly! But I really love this quilt. The flowers and the cake are from our daughter's wedding. Jim designed the cake. Wow, it was beautiful!

Jan Shore

169

Skill level: Intermediate

Block size sewn into quilt: 8-1/4" x 8-1/4" checkerboard, 8" x 16" basket

Number of blocks: 91 (88 checkerboard, 3 basket)

Finished quilt size: 94-3/4" x 114"

SUPPLIES

Note: Yardage is based on 42" wide cotton fabric.
- 1/4 yd. of lavender tonal
- 3/8 yd. of gold tonal
- 5/8 yd. of green tonal
- 7/8 yd. each of deep pink tonal, dark pink tonal, medium pink tonal, light pink tonal, and pale pink tonal
- 1-1/4 yds. of yellow tonal
- 3-1/4 yd. of mottled light blue
- 5-1/4 yds. of mottled cream
- 103" x 122" piece of backing
- 103" x 122" piece of batting
- 3-1/2 yds. of 18" wide fusible web
- Thread in colors to match fabrics
- Rotary cutter, ruler, and mat
- Template plastic
- Basic sewing and pressing supplies

CUTTING INSTRUCTIONS

From the gold tonal, cut:
One 5-1/4" x 42" strip; recut into three 5-1/4" squares, then cut diagonally in half *twice*; and three 47/8" squares
One 3-3/8" x 42" strip; recut into six 3-3/8" squares

From the deep pink tonal, cut:
Seven 3-1/4" x 42" strips (for strip sets)
Three 1-3/4" squares

From the dark pink tonal, cut:
Seven 3-1/4" x 42" strips (for strip sets)
Three 2-3/4" squares; cut diagonally in half *twice*

From the medium pink tonal, cut:
Seven 3-1/4" x 42" strips (for strip sets)
Six 2-3/8" squares; cut diagonally in half *once*

From the light pink tonal, cut:
Seven 3-1/4" x 42" strips (for strip sets)
Three 4-1/2" squares; cut diagonally in half *twice*

From the pale pink tonal, cut:
Six 3-7/8" squares; cut diagonally in half *once*
Seven 3-1/4" x 42" strips (for strip sets)

From the yellow tonal, cut:
One 3-3/8" x 42" strip; recut into twelve 3-3/8" squares

From the mottled light blue, cut:
Three 16-1/2" x 32-1/2" strips
Two 13-7/8" x 40-1/2" strips
One 8-7/8" x 42" strip; recut into three 8-7/8" squares
Two 8-1/2" x 40-1/2" strips

From the mottled cream, cut:
Thirty-three 3-1/4" x 42" strips (for strip sets)
Fifteen 2-1/2" x 42" strips (for sashing and border)
Eleven 2-1/4" x 42" strips (for binding)

INSTRUCTIONS

Note: Use a 1/4" seam allowance throughout. Press seams toward the darker fabric after adding each piece or as indicated.

Checkerboard Section Assembly

1. Following **Diagram 1** and using 3-1/4" x 42" strips, sew a mottled cream strip lengthwise between two pink tonal strips. (**Note:** Select hues of pink tonal in a random manner for strip sets. Two pink tonal strips will be left over after all strip sets are created. Discard.) Make a total of 11 strip sets. In the same manner, stitch a pink tonal strip lengthwise between two mottled cream strips. Make a total of 11 strip sets. Crosscut one hundred thirty-two 3-1/4" wide pink/cream/pink segments and one hundred thirty-two 3-1/4" wide cream/pink/cream segments.

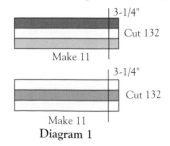

Diagram 1

2. Referring to the **Checkerboard Block Diagrams**, sew a cream/pink/cream segment between two pink/cream/pink segments to make one Block A. Press seams toward the outer segments. Make a total of 44 A blocks. Stitch a pink/cream/pink segment between two cream/pink/cream segments to make one Block B. Press seams toward the center segment. Make a total of 44 B blocks.

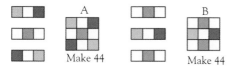

Checkerboard Block Diagrams

3. Sew six A blocks alternately together with five B blocks to make one A row as shown in **Diagram 2**. Press seams toward the A blocks. Make a total of four A rows. Stitch six B blocks alternately together with five A blocks to make one B row. Press seams toward the A blocks. Make a total of four B rows. Following the **Quilt Layout Diagram**, sew two A rows alternately together with two B rows to complete one 33-1/2" x 91-1/4" checkerboard section. Press seams in one direction. Repeat to make a second section.

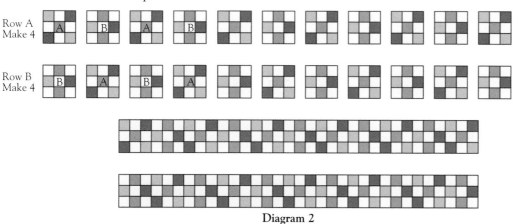

Diagram 2

Basket Section Assembly

1. Draw a diagonal line on the wrong side of each 4-7/8" gold tonal square. Following **Diagram 3**, place a marked square on one corner of each 8-7/8" mottled light blue square. Sew on the drawn lines, trim 1/4" beyond the lines, and press the triangles open. Cut each unit diagonally in half through the triangle to yield a total of three base units and three reverse base units.

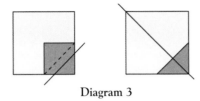

Diagram 3

2. Referring to the **Basket Block Diagrams**, stitch four 3-3/8" yellow tonal squares together with two 3-3/8" gold tonal squares and four gold tonal triangles into rows. Sew the rows together. Stitch a base unit to one short side and a reverse base unit to the other short side to complete one block. Make a total of three basket blocks.

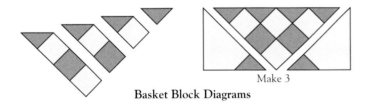

Make 3

Basket Block Diagrams

3. Sew a 16-1/2" x 32-1/2" mottled light blue strip to the top of each basket block as shown in **Diagram 4**. Press seams toward the strips.

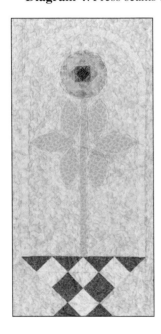

Make 3

Diagram 4

4. Following the **Quilt Layout Diagram**, stitch the three basket strip units alternately together with the two 8-1/2" x 40-1/2" mottled light blue strips. Press seams toward the blue strips. Sew a 13-7/8" x 40-1/2" mottled light blue strip to each side to complete the 40-1/2" x 91-1/4" basket section. Press seams toward the blue strips.

Appliqué

1. *Roses.* Following **Diagram 5**, sew a dark pink tonal triangle to each side of a 1-3/4" deep pink tonal square. Press seams away from the square. Stitch a medium pink tonal triangle to each side of the unit. Repeat first with light pink triangles and then with pale pink triangles. Make a total of three rose units. Cut three 6" squares from the fusible web. Center and fuse a square onto the wrong side of each rose unit, according to manufacturer's directions. Use the circle pattern provided to make a template. Cut out neatly. Position the template on the center of each rose unit and then cut out neatly to complete the roses.

Make 3
Diagram 5

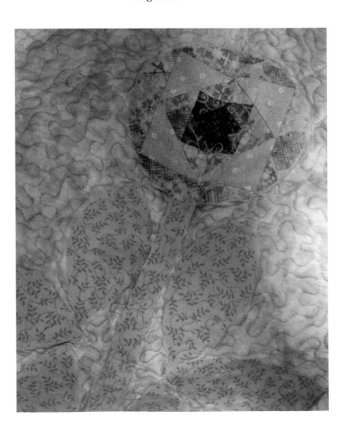

2. Cut two 5" x 18" strips and two 2-1/2" x 18" strips from the fusible web. Fuse the 5" wide strips onto the wrong side of the lavender tonal fabric, then cut eight 4-1/4" squares for diamonds. Fuse the 2-1/2" wide strips onto the wrong side of the green tonal fabric, then cut three 3/4" x 21-1/2" strips for stems.

3. Using the patterns provided, trace the basket handles onto the paper side of the remaining fusible web. Trace the leaves inside the handles to conserve fusible web, leaving at least 1/2" between shapes. Cut out roughly. Fuse the handles onto the wrong side of the remaining yellow tonal fabric and the leaves onto the wrong side of the remaining green tonal fabric. Cut out neatly. Remove the paper backing.

4. Referring to the photo for placement, arrange the lavender squares on the light blue strips in the basket section. Fuse in place. Arrange the remaining shapes, including the roses and stems, on the basket strips. Fuse in place. Stitch all shapes in place using matching thread.

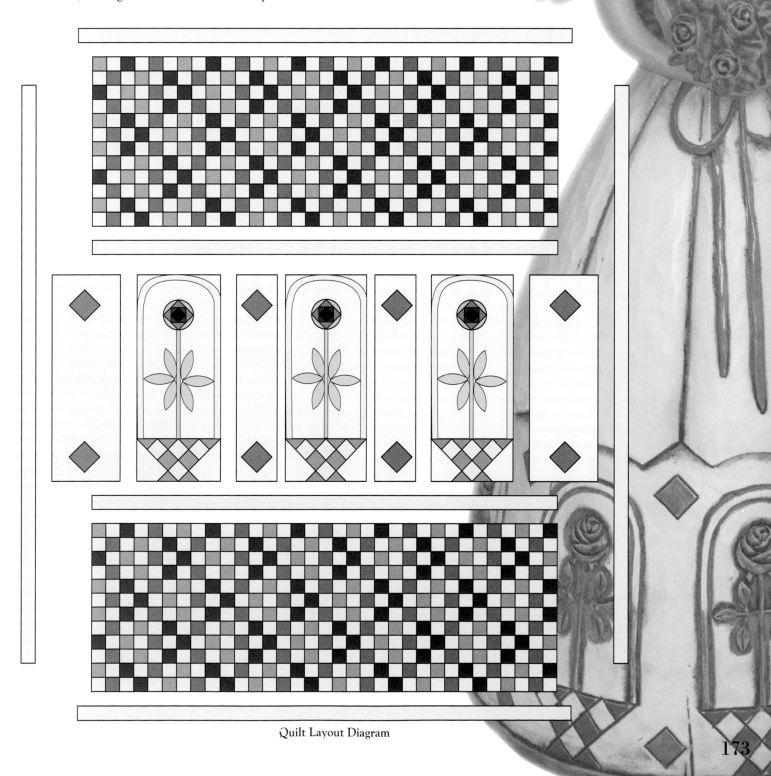

Quilt Layout Diagram

173

Quilt Assembly and Finishing

1. Sew the fifteen 2-1/2" x 42" mottled cream strips short ends together to make one long strip. Press seams in one direction. Cut two 91-1/4" lengths, two 110-1/2" lengths, and two 95-1/4" lengths. Referring to the **Quilt Layout Diagram**, stitch the checkerboard sections and basket section alternately together with the 2-1/2" x 91-1/4" strips to complete the quilt center.

2. *Border*. Sew the 2-1/2" x 110-1/2" mottled cream strips to the sides of the quilt center. Press seams toward the border. Stitch the 2-1/2" x 95-1/4" mottled cream strips to the top and bottom. Press seams toward the border.

3. Layer the quilt top right side up on top of the batting and the wrong side of the backing. Quilt as desired. Trim backing and batting even with the quilt top.

4. Bind as desired using the eleven 2-1/4" x 42" mottled cream strips.

Jim Shore's hand drawing of quilt. ©JSHORE

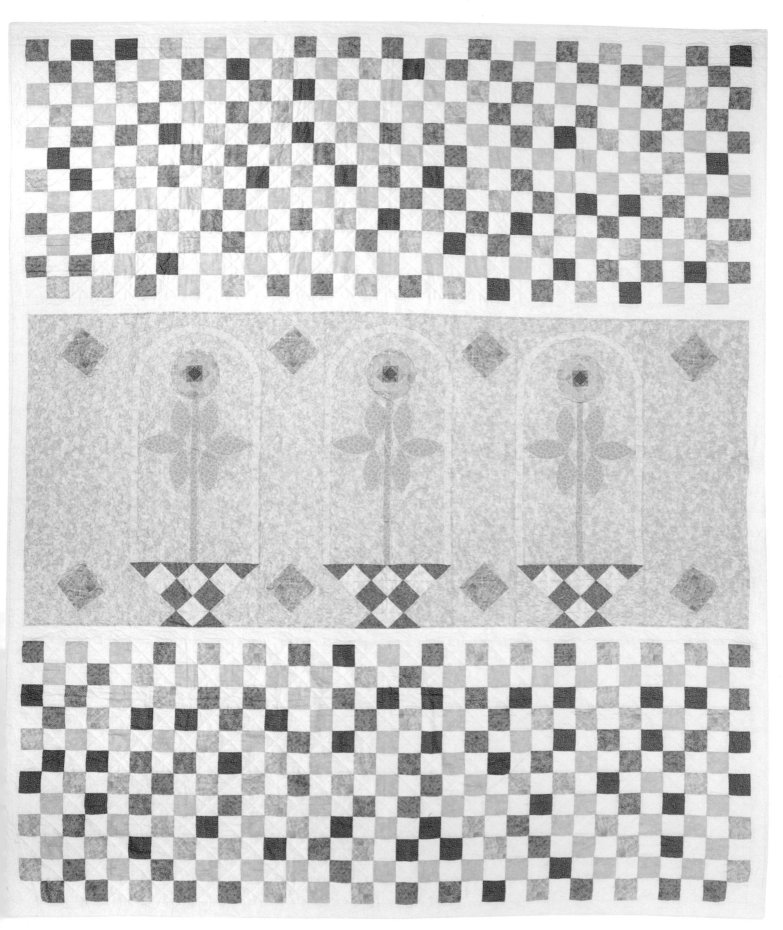

Designed by Jan Shore • **Pieced by Sandy Boobar** • **Finished quilt size:** 94-3/4" x 114"

General Quilting Instructions

Quilt	Approximate Size
Baby Quilt	36" x 54"
Lap Throw	54" x 72"
Twin	54" x 90"
Double	72" x 90"
Queen	90" x 108"
King	108" x 108"

Metric Conversion Chart		
1/8" = 3 mm	1" = 2.5 cm	7" = 17.8 cm
1/4" = 6 mm	2" = 5.1 cm	8" = 20.3 cm
1/2" = 1.3 cm	3" = 7.6 cm	9" = 22.9 cm
3/4" = 1.9 cm	4" = 10.2 cm	10" = 25.4 cm
7/8" = 2.2 cm	5" = 12.7 cm	11" = 27.9 mm
	6" = 15.2 cm	12" = 30.5 mm

1/8 yd. = 0.11 m	1/2 yd. = 0.46 m
1/4 yd. = 0.23 m	3/4 yd. = 0.69 m
1/3 yd. = 0.3 m	1 yd. = 0.91 m

Approximate Conversion To Metric Formula

When you know:		Multiply by:		To find:
inches (")	x	25	=	millimeters (mm)
inches (")	x	2.5	=	centimeters (cm)
inches (")	x	0.025	=	meters (m)
feet (' or ft.)	x	30	=	centimeters (cm)
feet (' or ft.)	x	0.3	=	meters (m)
yards (yd.)	x	90	=	centimeters (cm)
yards (yd.)	x	0.9	=	meters (m)

Before beginning, read the directions for the chosen pattern in their entirety. Wash all fabric in the manner in which you intend to wash the finished quilt. This preshrinks the fabric and ensures that it is colorfast. Dry fabric and press to remove wrinkles.

Most fabrics are sold as 44" wide from selvedge to selvedge, but many vary slightly in width. Fabric width may also change after the fabric is washed. The materials lists and cutting directions in this book are based on a width of at least 42" of useable fabric after washing and after the selvedges have been trimmed.

Backing fabric and batting dimensions listed are for hand quilting or for quilting on a home sewing machine. Professional quilters using a longarm machine may require a larger backing and batting size. If you intend to have someone else quilt your project, consult them regarding backing and backing size. Cut backing fabric and sew pieces together as necessary to achieve the desired size.

Patterns

The patterns provided for pieced quilts are full size with an included ¼" seam allowance. The solid line is the cutting line, and the dashed line is the stitching line. A seam allowance is not included on appliqué patterns. Trace all, including any grainline arrows, onto template material.

Marking Fabric Pieces

Test marking pens and pencils for removability before marking pieces for your quilt. If the pattern piece includes a grainline arrow, align the arrow with the fabric grain. Use your marker to trace around the template on the right side of the fabric. Then cut the pieces out.

If you wish to mark the sewing line, use a quilter's ¼" ruler to measure and mark the seam allowance on the wrong side of the fabric. Mark the pieces needed to complete one block, cut them out, and stitch them together before cutting pieces for the entire quilt.

Trace appliqué patterns lightly on the right side of the fabric or place the templates face down on the wrong side of the fabric. Add the seam allowance specified in the pattern when cutting the fabric pieces out.

Piecing

Set up your machine to sew 12 stitches per inch. If you have not marked the stitching line on fabric pieces, be careful to align fabric edges with the marks on the throat plate of your machine, as necessary, to achieve an accurate ¼" seam allowance. You can also make a stitching guide in the following way: Place a ruler under the presser foot of the sewing machine aligning the ¼" marked line on the ruler with the needle. Align a piece of masking tape or a rectangle cut from a moleskin footpad along the right edge of the ruler. Remove the ruler, and place fabric edges against the stitching guide as you sew. Stitch fabric pieces from edge to edge unless directed otherwise in the pattern.

Sew fabric pieces together in the order specified in the pattern. Wherever possible, press seam allowances toward the darkest fabric. When butting seams, press seam allowances in opposing directions.

Fusible Appliqué

This method allows you to complete appliqué very quickly. Follow the directions on the fusible product to prepare and attach appliqué pieces. For most fusible products, it is necessary to flip asymmetrical templates right side down before tracing them on the paper side of the fusible web. Finish the edges of fused appliqué pieces by hand using a blanket stitch or by machine using either a blanket or satin stitch.

Foundation Piecing

Foundation patterns are full size and do not include seam allowances. Trace the foundation patterns onto foundation paper making the number of foundations specified in the quilt pattern. You will piece each foundation in numerical order, placing fabric pieces on the unmarked side of the foundation, then turning the foundation over and stitching on the marked lines. Cut each fabric piece large enough to extend at least ¼" beyond the stitching lines of the section it will cover after it is stitched.

Begin by placing the first fabric piece right side up over section 1 on the unmarked side of the foundation. Hold the foundation up to a light source to better see the marked lines. Place the second piece of fabric right side down over the first piece. Pin fabrics in place if desired. Turn the foundation over and stitch on the line between section 1 and section 2 extending the stitching by two or three stitches on each end of the marked line. Fold the paper foundation along the stitched line so that the seam allowance of the stitched pieces extends beyond the paper. Align the ¼" line of a ruler along the stitches and trim the seam allowance to ¼". Open up the paper, flip the fabric pieces open, and press the unit. Continue adding fabric pieces in the same manner as the second fabric piece until the entire foundation is covered. Trim fabrics ¼" beyond the edges of the foundation. Stitch foundations together as described in the quilt pattern using the paper foundations as a stitching guide. Gently remove foundation paper when instructed to do so in the quilt pattern.

Mitering Border Corners

Fold a border strip in half crosswise to determine the center. Match the center of the border to the center of the quilt, and pin the border to the quilt. Stitch the border to the quilt, beginning and ending exactly ¼" from the quilt edges. Backstitch to secure the stitching at each end. Attach all four borders in the same manner.

Place the quilt right side down on a flat surface, and place one border over the adjacent border as shown. Using a ruler, draw a line at a 45° angle from the inner edge of the uppermost border to the outside edge. Reverse the positions of the borders and repeat to mark a second line. Mark all borders in the same manner.

Pin each set of adjacent borders right sides together along the marked lines. Stitch on the lines from the inner to the outer edge. Backstitch at each edge to secure the seam. Turn the quilt over and check each mitered seam. Trim the seam allowances to ¼".

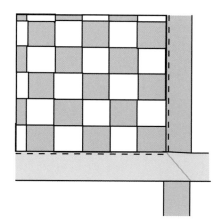

Marking the Quilt Top

Press the quilt top. Test all markers for removability before using them on your quilt. If using a paper design, place it under the quilt top, and trace the design. Use a light source if necessary. If using a stencil, place it on top of the quilt top, and trace the open areas. Use a ruler to mark straight lines such as grids or diagonals that cross fabric pieces.

Masking tape can be used as an alternative to marking straight lines. Place the tape on the quilt where desired and stitch along the edge. Contact paper can be cut into strips and used in the same manner. It can also be cut into other quilting shapes or stencils. Remove tape and contact paper from the quilt top daily to avoid leaving a sticky residue on the quilt.

Basting

The day before you intend to baste the quilt, open up the batting and place it on a flat surface (a bed or carpeted area is ideal). The next day, place the pressed backing fabric wrong side up on a flat, solid surface. Secure the backing in place with masking tape. Smooth the batting on top of the backing. Center the quilt top right side up on the batting.

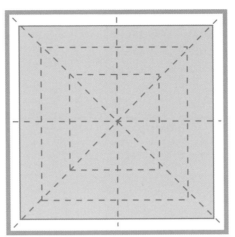

Use a needle and thread in a color that contrasts with the quilt. Baste with large stitches keeping all knots on top of the quilt. Begin in the quilt center and baste first horizontally, then vertically, and finally diagonally to the edge of the quilt top. Also baste at least two rectangles as shown.

To prepare your quilt for quilting on your home sewing machine: Use soluble thread to baste the quilt, or baste using safety pins.

Quilting

Many fine books are available on both hand and machine quilting. Basic hand quilting is described here.

Use quilting thread and a short, strong needle. Place a thimble on the middle finger of your preferred hand. Always begin quilting in the center of the quilt and work your way toward the quilt edge. Make a small knot at the end of the thread, and insert the threaded needle into the quilt top and batting only near where you wish your first quilting stitch to appear. Exit the needle at the beginning of where you want your first visible stitch to be, and gently pop the knot between the fabric fibers into the quilt top.

Begin quilting as follows: Keeping your preferred hand above the quilt and your other hand below it, use your thimbled finger to push the needle straight down through all layers of the

quilt. When you feel the tip of the needle with the index or middle finger of the hand that is below the quilt, use the thumb of your preferred hand to depress the quilt top, and redirect the needle back through the quilt layers to the top of the quilt. Continue in this manner using a rocking motion with your preferred hand. When the thread becomes short, make a small knot at the surface of the quilt top. Then take a stitch and pop the knot into the quilt. Cut the thread where it exits the quilt top. Do not remove basting stitches until quilting is complete.

Binding Strips

Quilts with straight edges can be bound with binding strips cut with the grain of the fabric. Cut binding strips the width specified in the quilt pattern, and sew them together with diagonal seams in the following way: Place two binding strips right sides together and perpendicular to each other, aligning the ends as shown. Mark a line on the top strip, from the upper left edge of the bottom strip to the lower right edge of the top strip, and stitch on the marked line. Trim the seam allowance ¼" beyond the stitching, open up the strips, and press the seam allowance open. When all binding strips have been stitched together, fold the strip in half lengthwise (wrong side in) and press.

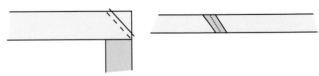

Bias Bindings

Quilts with curved edges must be bound with binding strips cut on the bias. Cut bias 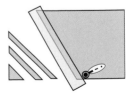 strips by aligning the 45° line on a rotary cutting ruler with the bottom edge of the fabric and cutting along the ruler's edge.

Attaching the Binding

Leaving at least 6″ of the binding strip free and beginning several inches away from a corner of the quilt top, align the raw edges of the binding with the edge of the quilt top. Using a standard ¼″ seam allowance, stitch the binding to the quilt, stopping and backstitching exactly ¼″ from the corner of the quilt top.

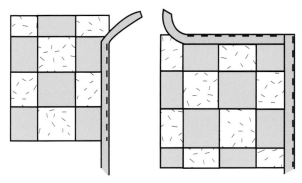

Remove the quilt from the sewing machine, turn the quilt so the stitched portion of the binding is away from you, and fold the binding away from the quilt, forming a 45° angle on the binding. *Hint: When the angle is correct, the unstitched binding strip will be aligned with the next edge of the quilt top.*

Maintaining the angled corner fold, fold the loose binding strip back down, aligning this fold with the stitched edge of the quilt top and the raw edge of the binding with the adjacent quilt top edge. Stitch the binding to the quilt beginning at the fold, backstitching to secure the seam.

Continue attaching the binding in the same manner until you are 6″ from the first stitching. Then, fold both loose ends of the binding strip back upon themselves so that the folds meet in the center of the unstitched section of the binding, and crease the folds.

Measure the width of the folded binding strip. Cut both ends of the binding strip that measurement beyond the creased folds. (For example: If the quilt pattern instructed you to cut the binding strips 2½″ wide, the folded binding strip would measure 1¼″. In this case, you would cut both ends of the binding strip 1¼″ beyond the creased folds.)

Open up both ends of the binding strip and place them right sides together and perpendicular to each other as shown. Mark a line on the top strip from the upper left corner of the top strip to the lower right corner of the bottom strip. Pin the strips together and stitch on the marked line.

Refold the binding strip and place it against the quilt top to test the length. Open the binding strip back up, trim the seam allowance ¼″ beyond the stitching, and finger press the seam allowance open. Refold the binding strip, align the raw edges with the edge of the quilt top, and finish stitching it to the quilt.

Trim the batting and backing ⅜″ beyond the binding stitching. Fold the binding to the back of the quilt, and blind stitch it to the backing fabric covering the machine stitching. Keep your stitches small and close together. When you reach a corner, stitch the mitered binding closed on the back side of the quilt, and pass the needle through the quilt to the right side. Stitch the mitered binding closed on the front side of the quilt, and pass the needle back through the quilt to the back side. Continue stitching the folded edge of the binding to the back of the quilt.

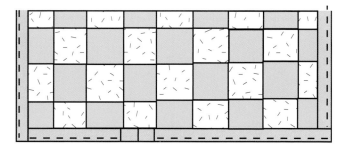

Finishing Your Quilt

Remove all quilt markings. Make a label that includes your name, the city where you live, the date the quilt was completed, and anything else you would like future owners of the quilt to know. Permanent fabric pens make this task easy and allow you to make the label as decorative as desired. Stitch the label to the back of the quilt.

Jim Shore and Kilburnie

Kilburnie, built in 1827 and the oldest surviving antebellum home in Lancaster, South Carolina, was designated to be demolished in 1999. The structure was saved from demolition by Dutch, born New Yorker Johannes Tromp, director of Windows on the World Restaurant in New York City.

Johannes and his partner John Craig rescued the building by disassembling the piazzas and two upper floors, and numbering all lumber for future re-assembly. The first floor was moved in one piece and placed upon a new foundation at historic Craig Farm, three and a half miles away from Kilburnie's original site. After a meticulous restoration, the home is now a successful, luxurious, and comfortable bed-and-breakfast, having earned a recommendation from *Southern Living Magazine* and having received many other accolades.

One of the biggest restoration challenges was the parlor's original 1834 elaborate ornamental plaster crown molding, highly unusual for this part of the country. The majority of the molding was missing and the remaining details were severely damaged by time, water, and vandalism.

This is where Jim Shore came into the picture and to the rescue. He stopped by one day during the restoration progress and showed much interest in the history of Kilburnie and the restoration process itself. Jim introduced himself to Johannes and they began a conversation about their mutual interest in restoration and preservation of historic buildings. Johannes took Jim on a tour through the entire building and when showing the parlor, Johannes lamented to Jim about his failed efforts to find a qualified craftsman to restore the parlor's elaborate crown moldings. Jim studied the remaining molding details for a while, then turned to Johannes, and simply stated "I'll do it for you". And "do it" he did. Jim first re-created each individual detail by sculpting them in clay and, from that, made high-definition molds. Jim than used ground-up pecan shells mixed with resin to re-create the hundreds of pieces required to remake the original crown molding in exacting detail. Jim, who beyond his artistic talents possesses a sophisticated engineering mind, identified 22 different wood moldings needed to re-create the original contour of the elaborate crown molding. Jim then glued each newly re-created detail fragment on the individual wood moldings, custom spacing them to accommodate the different lengths needed on each wall.

Guests arriving at Kilburnie are always immediately taken by the beautiful and elaborate crown moldings, re-created by Jim, in both the parlor and dining room of Kilburnie.

Jim's enthusiasm in the Kilburnie restoration project did not stop there; he also painted a life-size painting of the young Andrew Jackson as a proud successful general right after the battle of New Orleans. The huge painting dominates the center stairwell of Kilburnie. Jim also painted portraits of George Washington; Andrew Jackson at an older age; William R. Davie, an Englishman who settled in the Waxhaws and later became governor of North Carolina, where he later founded the Davie University; and a 1791 scene depicting George Washington visiting Barr's tavern in Lancaster.

This latter painting also reveals Jim's sense of humor. He painted himself in to the scene; seated on some rocks, he is seen sketching the historic moment on parchment for prosperity. His son Michael, who was seven years old at the time, is standing right next to him. Jim also painted the faces of Johannes, John Craig, and Paul Belk (the contractor) in the scene. While Jim has not acknowledged it, Johannes also recognizes Jim's wife Jan and one of his daughters in the painting. It is up to the viewer to decide who is who in the picture.

The Shore family is now a special part of the history of Kilburnie. Jim has even hidden a surprise behind the molding to be discovered by a distant future generation of restorers. Word has it that it is an envelope with Jim's writing, along with photographs and newspaper clippings about Kilburnie. Johannes and Jim have become great friends over the years. Jim's daughter

Robin was married on Kilburnie soil, marking that ground sacred to her. Jim and his wife Jan have spent nights in their favorite hideout, the Walkup Suite, which is a large luxurious attic suite with exposed beams. During one of those stays, the floor was just littered with many of Jim's sketches bursting with new ideas for future sculpted figures.

It has been Kilburnie and Johannes Tromp's honor to have Jim and Jan's book photographed at Kilburnie. Hopefully, the beauty of this special place will shine through the photos as the quilter reads these pages.

Special Thanks

My special thanks also to the following people:

To Jim Shore, my wonderful and long-suffering husband, who has constantly encouraged and supported me. Jim's incredible designs and artwork are the heart of this entire book. I love you and keep designing—I'm seeing another book in our future.

To Kathy (Billie) Atwell, who has worked with me from the initial concept and has designed several of the quilts in this book.

To Johannes Tromp for allowing us the run of Kilburne House Bed & Breakfast and his home.

To Gerald Massie for all his help with editing and friendship.

To Rosalind Walshe for her help with the photo styling and book layout, and her pushing and prodding.

To Iva Mintz and the Piece Makers Quilt Guild who brought my designs to life.

To Cyndi Andrews and The White House. She opened her fabric resources to me and has been there constantly to offer help.

Jan Shore